What a great read Lee Eclov has given us—it's readable, inspirational, and practical. The title of the first chapter pretty much says it all: "You Can't Feel at Home in an Organization." With all the past church emphasis on leadership, management, and organizational theory, it's easy to forget what the church has been called to do, that is to create a family environment where God's people, using their God-given talents and abilities, can share the gospel. In these circumstances evangelism becomes second nature, not a duty that makes many break out in a cold sweat. There's good theory here and lots of practical tips you can use to make your church feel like home. Give it a try.

BOB RUSSELL

Retired Senior Minister, Southeast Christian Church; author of *After Fifty Years of Ministry*

It's one thing to pay lip service to the idea of church as a family. It's another thing entirely to reorient every part of a church around this perspective. Drawing on a lifetime of faithful pastoral ministry, Lee Eclov challenges contemporary assumptions and paints a compelling real-life picture of church as a true home. I pray that its beauty moves more leaders to boldly recapture a vision for pastoral parenting.

ANGELA J. WARD

Ministry author and teacher; writer at Church Matters; host of the Church Chat podcast

What a refreshing book! Imagine a church whose primary emphasis is to make people "feel at home." This book is more desperately needed than ever in a day when the nuclear family is falling apart and people are seeking meaningful connections and fellowship. In short, they are seeking for a family. I wish every young pastor could read this book and be liberated from the need to keep up to date with the latest insights on church growth, church management, and church messaging. All these are important, but there is no substitute for attending a church that makes you feel at home. Thanks, Lee, for a wonderful reminder of what the church is to be.

ERWIN W. LUTZER

Pastor Emeritus, The Moody Church, Chicago

In my first groggy moments after waking up in an unfamiliar bed on vacation, nothing is more reassuring and clarifying than my wife's voice saying, "Remember, you're in a hotel room." Weary church leaders will experience a similar reaction to Lee Eclov's crucial refrain in this book: "Remember, your church is a home." By drawing liberally from Scripture and his considerable pastoral experience, Eclov replaces dry, corporate metaphors for ministry with warm, encouraging—but never overly saccharine—stories of God's people as a family. I especially appreciate the thoughtful and creative ways he implements these biblical concepts in his own congregation. Eclov's pastoral heart beats on every page. I never felt like I was "eating my veggies," but I know my understanding of church life is healthier having read this book.

KYLE ROHANE

Editor, CTPastors

Too many books on pastoral ministry set Christian leaders up to fail by promoting scale over substance, success over faithfulness. Not so in Lee Eclov's *Feels Like Home*. In this excellent book, Pastor Lee reminds ministry leaders that their job is not to be CEOs of successful companies, but to lead a family of believers with Christlike love. Let this book teach, inspire, and challenge you as it did me. Most of all, let it remind you that God calls every Christian leader to be a "homemaker."

JARED E. ALCÁNTARA

Associate Professor of Preaching, George W. Truett Seminary, Baylor University

A book about the church being a family—that's not a new idea. But such a book that is not clinical or therapeutic or theological, but like a father running hard, arms flung wide, to welcome home his wayward son— maybe that's not new either, but it's fresh, beautiful, wise, and healing. *Feels Like Home* feels, well, like home. Lee Eclov writes like a father who's just ordered the fattened calf served up, and whose feet are already tapping to fiddle music. Come on in! There's bread to spare here, and then some.

MARK BUCHANAN
Author of *Your Church Is Too Safe*; speaker, pastor, professor

In today's culture, we're tempted to think of church as a business, a mission, or a performing arts venue. Lee Eclov reminds us that the Bible refers to believers primarily as God's household, a family! That makes a big difference in how we lead this group of brothers and sisters we're called into. We all know the highest praise we can hear from someone new to the church is not, "I'm aligned with the cause" or "I love the music," but "I've found a home!" Lee, well said and well led, brother.

MARSHALL SHELLEY
Director of the Doctor of Ministry program at Denver Seminary

After a generation of leadership coaching in the church based on business principles, Lee Eclov invites us to renew our vision of congregational life built on relationship. His warm writing style is born out of decades of pastoral ministry that flows from his deep, foundational conviction that church is meant first and foremost to be a family—not in name only, but because we are learning to live the life of Jesus together. *Feels Like Home* is filled with practical examples and solid scriptural counsel designed to recalibrate our vision of the local church.

MICHELLE VAN LOON
Author of *Born to Wander: Recovering the Value of Our Pilgrim Identity*

Amidst a culture that increasingly views church as an industrial complex, Lee Eclov's invitation to regain the biblical vision of church as a family is a refreshing reminder of God's gracious initiation of adoption. Framed by decades of pastoral experience, Lee draws from both anecdotal and exegetical insight to beckon the bride of Christ back to its first calling: making a home for prodigals to return to. Full of wisdom from a spiritual father, *Feels Like Home* is a timely challenge for churches everywhere who long to see their communities of faith transformed into reunions of brothers and sisters reconciled to the Father.

STEPHEN L. WOODWORTH
Associate Coordinator of International Theology Education Network (ITEN)
Evangelical Presbyterian Church (EPC): World Outreach

Too often we pastors don't see the human faces of those we are called to shepherd. We see blocs, masses, and groups. So people coming into our churches feel like they are entering a factory or an assembly line. This is why Lee Eclov's work is so important. Lee calls pastors to remember their first calling as shepherds and reminds us that we are not merely individual Christians but members of a family, and that when we gather together, we are coming home. Many people coming into our churches are looking for a family, looking to belong, and looking for a home. What makes this book so good is that Lee is writing from a lifetime of living out these ideas. I've visited his church and know that Lee puts into practice what he is teaching here. He's a shepherd who has been welcoming God's people home for many years. I wish every fresh-faced seminary graduate would stop what they are doing and read this book in its entirety.

DAN DARLING
Vice-President, Ethics and Religious Liberty Commission; author, *The Dignity Revolution*

I warmly commend Lee's winsome book, *Feels Like Home*, to anyone who is looking for a healthy alternative to big-box, institutional Christianity. Lee has done a wonderful job of making a deeply *relational* ecclesiology accessible to all levels of readers. *Feels Like Home* is a well-written, engaging book that speaks to the head as well as to the heart.

JOE HELLERMAN
Professor of New Testament Language and Literature, Talbot School of Theology

Lee Eclov

How Rediscovering the Church as Family Changes Everything

Feels Like Home

MOODY PUBLISHERS

CHICAGO

Some names and details in stories have been changed to protect the privacy of individuals.

All Scripture quotations, unless otherwise indicated, are taken from the Holy Bible, New International Version®, NIV®. Copyright © 1973, 1978, 1984, 2011 by Biblica, Inc.™ Used by permission of Zondervan. All rights reserved worldwide. www.zondervan.com. The "NIV" and "New International Version" are trademarks registered in the United States Patent and Trademark Office by Biblica, Inc.™

Scripture quotations marked ESV are from The Holy Bible, English Standard Version® (ESV®), copyright © 2001 by Crossway, a publishing ministry of Good News Publishers. Used by permission. All rights reserved.

Scripture quotations marked *The Message* are taken from THE MESSAGE, copyright © 1993, 2002, 2018 by Eugene H. Peterson. Used by permission of NavPress. All rights reserved. Represented by Tyndale House Publishers, Inc.

All emphasis in Scripture has been added.

Edited by Elizabeth Cody Newenhuyse
Interior and cover design: Erik M. Peterson
Cover photo of photo borders copyright © 2017 by SetsukoN/iStock (871398558).
Cover photo of worship copyright © 2018 by Athena Grace / Lightstock (192739).
Cover photo of Bible study at night copyright © 2018 by Pearl/Lightstock (73279).
Cover photo of Bible study in sunlight copyright © 2018 by Pearl/Lightstock (150836).
Cover photo of wood texture by Andrew Buchanan on Unsplash.
All rights reserved for all of the above photos.
Author photo: Magen Davis

Library of Congress Cataloging-in-Publication Data

Names: Eclov, Lee, author.
Title: Feels like home : how rediscovering the church as family changes
  everything / Lee Eclov.
Description: Chicago : Moody Publishers, 2019. | Includes bibliographical
  references.
Identifiers: LCCN 2019001471 (print) | LCCN 2019011384 (ebook) | ISBN
  9780802497581 (ebook) | ISBN 9780802418869
Subjects: LCSH: Church. | Family--Religious aspects--Christianity.
Classification: LCC BV600.3 (ebook) | LCC BV600.3 .E335 2019 (print) | DDC
  253--dc23
LC record available at https://lccn.loc.gov/2019001471

ISBN: 978-0-8024-1886-9

We hope you enjoy this book from Moody Publishers. Our goal is to provide high-quality, thought-provoking books and products that connect truth to your real needs and challenges. For more information on other books and products that will help you with all your important relationships, go to www.moodypublishers.com or write to:

Moody Publishers
820 N. La Salle Boulevard
Chicago, IL 60610

1 3 5 7 9 10 8 6 4 2

Printed in the United States of America

Dedicated to my church family,
the brothers and sisters, young and old,
of the Village Church of Lincolnshire

Contents

Foreword

What does home feel like to you? As a conversation starter, I like to ask new and old friends to describe that feeling and place.

I know just the place in my mind. It's the afternoon on Christmas, and I'm sitting on the floor in the living room of my Grandpa and Grandma Daniel's house. They lived on the farm just down the road from where I grew up in rural South Dakota. Grandpa has tossed logs in the fireplace. Snow falls in the backyard. Grandma has baked her famous spritz cookies. Presents pile up underneath the tree. And I'm surrounded by people who know and love me: along with my Grandma and Grandpa, I can see my parents, my brother, my aunt and uncle, and my cousins. I don't know how I could be happier.

But that place is gone. Another family now makes their own memories in the old farm house. Grandpa has long since succumbed to cancer and gone to be with Jesus. My brother has his own family hundreds of miles away. I have my own family hundreds of miles in another direction. I'll never see that scene again.

I've tried to give my children that feeling of home in our new house. This Christmas, we opened presents with both sets of their grandparents. It was lovely. I hope they cherish these memories and this place the way I did the old white farmhouse in South Dakota.

But I have an even greater hope for my children. I hope our church feels to them like home. I hope those people will be to them a family who loves them through every stage and situation of life. I hope they'll feel safe, welcome, and known by the members of this church as brothers and sisters in Christ. I hope they'll see this bond of the Spirit as even stronger than the bond their mother and I share with them by blood.

Apart from my children, I don't live within 650 miles of anyone who shares my DNA. I'll never again celebrate Christmas in that living room in South Dakota. But I'm surrounded by family. And I have a home. Even better, it's a home that fills me with longing for the home we'll share for eternity with God.

I don't always get along with everyone in this home, our church. Sometimes I hurt them with my words, or my lack of care. In some situations we don't agree on the best way forward. So we argue. Usually I need to apologize. Many of these brothers and sisters I've never even met, since this church family has grown so much in the last few years. And these aren't necessarily the first folks with whom I'd choose to spend my time. Some of us don't share many common interests. It really is a family.

When I read Lee Eclov, it's like he's been in my home. And that's not just because we both hail from South Dakota and crossed paths in the Chicago suburbs. It's because I share his vision of the church as a home. I've been in large churches and small churches, growing churches and dying churches, churches full of farmers and churches full of hipsters. Every church should work toward the vision Eclov lays out in *Feels*

Like Home: How Rediscovering the Church as Family Changes Everything.

This vision is not only biblical, but also attainable for every church. You don't have to be brilliant or rich or savvy or trendy. You could be declining and aging. You could be in the West or the Majority World. It doesn't matter. You can pray together. You can remember names. You can bring a meal. You can mourn with those who mourn. You can sing the songs that have sustained the faith of family members for generations.

Because in Christ, you have fellowship stronger than a brother's bond. You have a home that neither death nor time nor anything else in all creation can take away from you. When you rediscover the church as family, it changes everything.

COLLIN HANSEN
Editorial Director, The Gospel Coalition

Introduction

W hen I moved up here," Faith told me, "I was asking and trusting God to give me a home, physically and spiritually." Faith was fresh out of graduate school and when she arrived in the northern suburbs of Chicago she knew she was not in Kansas anymore. "As I sent my parents back to Kansas on Amtrak I began to pray desperately for the second home."

On her first Sunday, she drove to a church thirty minutes away, only to find that there was no one there for the advertised early service. After Googling, she drove to another church closer to her apartment. When she arrived she realized it was one campus of a megachurch, and her heart sank. It was too large. She Googled again and saw that our church was nearby. "As I sat in the parking lot of this, the third church of the morning, I was still fearful. What if I didn't fit in this new home? What was this church even like?

"What I was expecting I don't truly know, but what I found when I walked through the doors was surprising. I heard the laughter first, saw the pie second, and felt peace third. I felt so overwhelmed that I had to write to calm myself. So, I sat in the foyer and wrote out a prayer as I listened to the community around me. Eventually Katerina and Stamati, who had come to sit down, introduced themselves. They introduced me to several others and even invited me to their home."

When Christians look for a church they are looking for a home. They don't just need a place where they like the music or preaching, or where their kids are happy. They *need* a home because Christian discovery and growth can't happen without one. The Bible knows nothing of Christians disconnected from other believers. Jesus' people are a family, "the household of God" (Eph. 2:19 ESV). The Christian life cannot be lived properly as a loner.

"I heard the laughter first, saw the pie second, and felt peace third."

You might think a church that feels like home would be easy, but actually it is a miracle. Christian love and Christlike service don't come naturally at all. Neither do praying together or welcoming those who don't seem to be like us. In fact, life with our Christian family is counterintuitive at every turn. Everything that makes a church feel like home depends on the Holy Spirit working wonders within and among us. We're prone to blurred vision, like thinking music matters more than knowing one another's names, or that big churches naturally accomplish more for the Lord than small ones. We think we can fast-track outreach or discipleship without the slow work of raising a spiritual family. But after we have rested our faith in Christ, our number one duty for Him is to "love one another."

What about those of us tasked with leading a church family? Church leadership requires a kind of parenting, which is why elders are expected to manage their own households well. After all, "If anyone does not know how to manage his own family, how can he take care of God's church?" (1 Timothy 3:5). Later I'll tell you about a family with thirty-six children, most of them adopted from six different countries! Parenting all those children into a loving family is pretty much like what church leaders must do if our church is to feel like home.

Too often, of course, the church does not feel like home. You've experienced it. I have too. Church families are never perfect, any more than the homes we grew up in. But often, church leaders aren't really trying to shape their congregations into the life of God's family. In Part One of this book, "Our Family Album," we will look at the extraordinary design for "God's household" in Scripture—our covenant relationships, the radical significance of being called brothers and sisters, and the recalibrated relationships that arise from our mutual commitment to Christ. In Part Two, "Interior Design: The Spiritual Art of Decorating a Church Home," we will explore the ministry spheres that especially make a church home.

Our goal is to find the God-given ways that our fellowship can truly become family and what keeps us from doing so. Because when we do feel like we're coming home on a Sunday—well, read what author Addie Zierman says. In her blog, she explains what it was like when she and her family finally left what she called The Big Church, "feeling more and more adrift in this ever-changing sea of strangers."

> I remember the week that we got into the car and looked at each other and knew that it was done—that we couldn't go back. The next week we drove to a church down the street, and we sat in the sanctuary . . . and how can I describe it except to say that I could breathe?

It isn't a perfect place—the church we go to now. You and I both know that such a church does not exist. But there is space for struggle, for questions, for failure and forgiveness and healing and transformation.

Sunday mornings, we stand in the foyer talking, and the oxygen is rivering through us all—and slowly, slowly we are putting down roots. We are taking deep breaths. We are growing deeper into ourselves and into the God who holds us and sustains us like rich soil, like abundant earth.[1]

That morning when Faith sat in our foyer she wrote a prayer: "Dear God . . . You are the one who brings us together, the one who breaks down our walls and barriers . . . Lord, if it is this church, then fill me with your Spirit here so that I might feel your love through these people you have called to your side . . . The joy I can feel here, as I watch those that you have gathered, I see your joy. Lord, bless the members of this church, and bless my interactions."

When Faith found a church family we gained the privilege of discipling her in Christ and, at the same time, being strengthened by her spiritual maturity and gifts. We gained a sister!

PART ONE

Our Family Album

"I have seder envy," wrote Mary Schmich, a popular columnist for the *Chicago Tribune*. "I'm stricken by this curious condition every year as my Jewish friends gather to eat and drink and tell the tale of the Jews' liberation from slavery in Egypt. . . . [T]here's something about Passover that makes me want to feel included. . . . However close we may be, however much life we share, when it comes to the essential identity of tribe, I am not a member. I do not belong. I never will."

It was Good Friday when I first read that column. That night our church would gather to celebrate the Lord's Supper and remember that by His death we share in His body and blood. "Mary," I thought, "Jesus answers 'seder envy' by inviting all who would accept Him as their Passover Lamb to celebrate not only this meal, but to someday dine with Him at the Wedding Supper of the Lamb."

Schmich wrote, "I once mentioned to a Jewish friend that it sometimes—not often, just sometimes—felt strange to feel so apart from so many of my friends. 'It's a religion, it's not a race,' he countered. 'Anyone can join.'"[1]

Our friend Laura met my mother many years ago when Mom came to visit us. Laura was captivated by Mom, whose name, Grace, fits her perfectly. Many times Laura said, "I want to join your family." But it is a most unusual family whom you can join simply because you wish to. Such is the family of God. Of course, seder envy or not, no one would actually want to join God's family unless God mercifully makes them homesick. Then, through the grace of the Lord Jesus Christ, the Father adopts us and we become His household, brothers and sisters together.

The church as *home* has always been a rich theme in our Bibles. It is something we all long for. Family. A place where they take you in and set a place for you at the table. It is something that, sadly, too many do not enjoy or have walked away from, like someone who forgets their address. Part of pastoral work, of church leadership, is drawing people back home.

1

You Can't Feel at Home in an Organization

It seemed simple enough. Our Elder Board asked an ad hoc committee to provide guidelines for hiring future pastoral staff. I chose not to be on the committee, feeling others could easily handle the project. When they began to meet, the chair, a management consultant, felt that the place to start was making sure the ministries of our church were properly aligned. They took the name Alignment Task Force. That's when things got complicated for me.

It's what healthy organizations do, I know. Align. Get everything and everyone going in the same direction as their stated mission. Shed the distractions. Refocus.

As our Associate Pastor, Michael, excitedly reported to me on the task force's developments I grew increasingly agitated. It started like a dark cloud, about the size of a fist, on the distant horizon. A storm was brewing in me. It's pretty simple: I don't like this stuff. Actually, I'm unreasonably suspicious of it. I grumbled in my journal, "What is with the power of diagrams and lines?" It all felt like some kind of corporate plastic and chrome to me. On the morning after one Elders' meeting, I wrote, "This morning I feel like I have seen my own resignation around the bend. Maybe it's the headache talking."

The weeks passed as I brooded and thrashed about. I was a pain about it all, especially to my Associate who bore the brunt of my frustrations. I was well aware that this process is endorsed by church leaders everywhere. But there was no motivation in it for me at all. Yet I didn't know what to offer as an alternative. I tried to pray through my frustrations, but it was slow going and I probably was just grumbling to myself at least half the time.

Then it dawned on me. This was so hard for me because in our alignment efforts there seemed to be a subtle but unmistakable way of thinking of the church primarily as an *organization*. I'm motivated as a pastor to help create the right kind of *environment* for a church to be healthy and effective. That environment, to me, is best described as a *home*. As a pastor, I'm a "homemaker."

Years ago the church I served in Pennsylvania was featured in a front-page article in the local paper's Sunday edition. There was a big picture of me in our modest multipurpose auditorium. The article described our growth and our fresh approach to worship. The reporter had asked me about the challenges of pastoring a larger church, and I'd lamented that sometimes I felt more like a CEO than a pastor. Over the next few days, there was some more public response about me being a CEO pastor in my plush executive office (anyone with this opinion had clearly never seen my office)! In the end, anyone who misunderstood that quote in the paper could have just talked with me about it and I would have heartily agreed that a CEO is not a good pastoral model, even though sometimes that role can't be avoided.

Thinking of a church as home changes a lot. A home is considerably different from an organization. Church leaders have to be very careful when we take our cues from companies, nonprofits, civic organizations, and the like. But when we conceive of our church as home our priorities shift. Names matter more than numbers. We invest in the high priority of loving one another as the precursor to loving the lost. We take on the inefficient responsibility of caring for individuals. We learn to leave the ninety-nine in order to search for one lost sheep. We worship differently when we worship as a family. And leaders shepherd their flock more as parents than executives.

"Members of His Household"

It has been right before our eyes in the Bible all along. Scores of references to "brothers and sisters," to God as our Father, to Jesus as both our Bridegroom and Elder Brother, to the essential loving unity of God's family, and to the household environment of holiness, spiritual nurture, and safety. Paul taught Timothy "how people ought to conduct themselves in *God's household*, which is the church of the living God . . ." (1 Tim. 3:15). He told the Ephesians, "You are no longer foreigners and strangers, but fellow citizens with God's people and also members of *his household*" (Eph. 2:19).

New Testament Greek uses the word *oíkos* to refer to God's people about a dozen times. For example, in Matthew

24:44–45 Jesus refers to Himself as the head of the house and His followers as His "household." Hebrews 3:6 says, "Christ is faithful as the Son over God's *house*. And we are his *house*, if indeed we hold firmly to our confidence and the hope in which we glory." Peter twice refers to the "family of believers" or "brotherhood" (ESV) with the Greek word *adelphotes* (1 Peter 2:17; 5:9). Translators may not use the word *home*, but it is obviously a suitable synonym for our Christian family.

Commentator Robert Banks wrote, "A whole cluster of terms from family life are applied to the Christian community. Some of these are among the most frequently used terms in Paul's vocabulary." He also says, "So numerous are these, and so frequently do they appear, that the comparison of the Christian community with a 'family' must be regarded as the most significant metaphorical usage of all."[1]

Almost always, as with Banks, the description of the church as God's family is regarded as a metaphor, like the bride, field, or temple. But it isn't really a metaphor at all. God's household is the very definition of the church. We're not *like* a household or family. We *are* one.

Pastor and writer Mark Buchanan affirms this: "Jesus is not ashamed to be called our brother. The Father gives us the Spirit of adoption through whom we cry, 'Abba!' Jesus asks who his mother and brother and sisters are, and answers they are those who do the Father's will. From the cross Jesus says to the disciple John and his mother Mary, 'Behold your son; behold your mother.' And he says that our loyalty to him must transcend biological attachments."[2]

Where Vision Gets Fuzzy

To think of church as a home rather than an organization changes the way we lead. For one thing, vision statements—which many churches wrestle with—aren't very important in most families. I know a vision statement can be useful, but they're overrated when it comes to church families. Marshall Shelley, former editor of *Leadership Journal,* captured the problem in a 2017 column for *Preaching Today:*

> Once upon a time, a leader decided his family needed his leadership. And leadership equals vision, right? He'd been raised in a home with a passion for reading, so he had a similar vision for his family: "Our family honors God by being people of the Word and of words." Sort of catchy, he thought. He envisioned evenings spent reading and telling stories.
>
> For a while, the vision fit. Child #1 loved listening to stories and developed a knack for telling stories with great detail.
>
> Child #2 complicated the picture. She didn't have Child #1's interest in books. She was a natural athlete, developed into an outstanding gymnast, and while tolerating the reading-and-story culture, wasn't fully engaged. Family conversations shifted from books to balance-beam routines and flyaway dismounts.
>
> Child #3 complicated the picture further. She was born with serious mental disabilities. Reading would never be within her experience; even learning to speak would prove impossible. Child #3 led the family into another world—medical centers, physical therapy, support groups for families of children with disabilities.
>
> Question: what takes priority—the vision or the people? For the family above (with whom I'm, uh, somewhat acquainted) telling those members who weren't "aligned with the vision" to find another family simply wasn't an option.
>
> No, the vision needed to be expanded to include the new

realities—the needs of all those God brought into the family. The family's vision enlarged: "To honor God through words, deeds, and presence." It was lived by each family member differently.

When a church's vision and the church's people clash, what's the answer? Sometimes it's adjusting the vision. A church, like a family, is at least partly defined by those God has placed within it.[3]

Every church has outliers—people who don't get with the program. They seem like a drag on our progress. Too needy, maybe; or stubborn, or immature. I've heard of churches who tell those who won't commit to their vision to take a hike. Find another church. It's hard to pull that off in a family. You not only take what you get, but you must love them, too.

I imagine every pastor knows what it is to watch the horizon along with the Father for prodigals, loved but long gone.

The people in a church, just as in a family, have a way of going off in odd, unexpected directions. Some turn out to be more remarkable than we ever bargained for, like gifted or lion-hearted kids, a credit to the family. Some live for a long time in the fog of finding themselves. There are some who break our hearts. I imagine every pastor knows what it is to watch the horizon along with the Father for prodigals, loved but long gone. With such unpredictable families it is hard for a church to stick to the vision.

The family members are the primary concern of a healthy home. So it is in the church. It sounds nearly heretical to say so, but the lost are not our first concern as church leaders nor as church members. Our first responsibility is God's household. Peter told elders, "Be shepherds of God's flock that is under your care" (1 Peter 5:2). Both the Old Testament prophets and the New Testament apostles spend almost all their ink addressing the hearts and relationships of God's people.

Opening Our Home to the Orphans Outside

I read about a remarkable family in West Virginia. Paul and Jeane Briggs have thirty-six children. *Thirty-six children!* Thirty-one of them are adopted from the United States as well as Mexico, Russia, Ukraine, Bulgaria, and Ghana. Paul and Jeane seek out hard-to-place older and special-needs kids. Jeane says, "It's not for everybody, but it's what my husband and I feel called to do by our faith."[4] I wasn't surprised to read that they are Christians.

Not many parents can open their homes so wide, but that's just what churches were born to do. Churches should have that kind of attitude toward the spiritual orphans, outcasts, and outlaws whom God brings to our attention.

But . . . so often we in our churches don't have that attitude. And that mindset, that indifference to the spiritually homeless outside our church doors, is what more than anything else keeps us from building a community that feels like a real family of God. After all, what if "they" don't fit in? Churches that pride themselves on their warm fellowship can easily forget to go out into the alleys and back roads to bring in the spiritually hungry and homeless.

It's sad how cold a "friendly" church can be. A church consultant told me once that most church people, regardless of whether their congregation is big or small, don't really want their church to get any bigger. They're afraid it won't feel like their home anymore. And getting bigger isn't really the goal of a church family (believe it or not). But effective outreach starts with a *healthy* church family.

A church consultant once told me that most church people don't really want their church to get any bigger. They're afraid it won't feel like their home anymore.

If we are to think of our church as *home* we must remember to be an *open* home, or we will fail to be the kind of family Jesus called us to be. Colossians 3:11 says, "Here there is no Gentile or Jew, circumcised or uncircumcised, barbarian, Scythian, slave or free, but Christ is all, and is in all." Yes, that kind of sibling blending is easier said than done—in the early church as in ours—but it is the mark of a healthy church home.

Two striking Bible stories illustrate the kind of family God calls us to be—Ruth, in the Old Testament, and Philemon, in the New. We'll get to them in chapters 2 and 5.

When a church family matures in Christlike *qualities* we naturally develop Christlike *concern* for the lost. A healthy church family creates a kind of gravitational pull toward the gospel. Or to put it another way, we become like salt, giving people a thirst for Jesus and light illuminating the way to Christ.

There were three kids in my family, and our friends often hung out at our house. Recently, I asked one of my sister's best friends—let's call her "Greta"—what our home meant to her. She wrote,

> My niece, who is now 40, asked me a few years back why I am so different than my sisters who share the same genetics and grew

up in the same house. So why am I quick to give a hug, wipe a tear, and offer encouraging words? My only thoughts were that I really grew up in two households, that of my parents (very stoic and undemonstrative) and YOUR household with parents that praised us, prayed with us and for us, and freely gave hugs. I remember needing to check in with your mom when we came home at night. Even if your folks were in bed, we knocked, went in, got a hug and maybe a quick prayer before we went to bed.

Contrast that to my place where I crept in as quietly as I could, not because I was past curfew but because I shouldn't disturb my parents at any time. Hugs? I got one from my mom as she was dying—sitting on the couch in horrible pain. And one from my dad when I flew home from Berlin on emergency leave from the military to visit him in St. Luke's after he had a major heart attack. I believe the praise, prayers, and hugs from your parents really did make a difference in my life.

Churches can be like that in the lives of people who yearn for a home for their hearts.

It Takes Time

Can you imagine that Briggs household with all those kids? Just a couple of kids can wear parents out. But parents have no choice but to take a long view of things. "She'll grow out of it," we tell each other on bad days. "She's growing up too fast," we say on good days. Still, growing, whether "out of" or "up," takes a long time. It's the same at church. When you're the pastor of a church *family* you had better learn to be patient. I have a clock on the wall of my office that I made from a broad, weathered piece of fence. In it, next to the clock face, I carved the words, "Things take time."

The beautiful thing—the real wonder, as any parent knows—is that children do grow up. Likewise, pastors watch infant believers become godly and wise. Some prodigals come home to the Father. Relationships heal as they should. Tiny seeds of faith grow into "oaks of righteousness" (Isa. 61:3). Captives walk free. Dispirited mourners are perfumed with joy and dressed in praise.

"God Sets the Lonely in Families"

Home is my favorite word. It undoubtedly started with my own family, a gift of God to me, but my many years of pastoral ministry have reinforced my belief that God embedded in our hearts a deep longing for family that not even the finest of earthly homes can satisfy.

For many people, of course, *home* is not a word resonant with warm memories. Terrible things happen in families. Parents abandon their kids. Home is not safe. Or, like Greta, we may recall our homes as cold and remote.

J. D. Vance, in his bestselling memoir, *Hillbilly Elegy*, writes about a former high school classmate. When she posted on Facebook that "she had finally found a man who would treat her well (a refrain I'd seen many times before), her thirteen-year-old daughter commented: 'Just stop. I just want you and this to stop.' I wish I could hug that little girl, because I know how she feels. For seven long years, I just wanted it to stop. I didn't care so much about the fighting, the screaming, or even the drugs. I just wanted a home, and I wanted to stay there. . . ."[5]

God designed the church to be home for people who feel like that. Psalm 68:4–6 says,

Sing to God, sing in praise of his name,
>   extol him who rides on the clouds;
>   rejoice before him—his name is the LORD.
A father to the fatherless, a defender of widows,
>   is God in his holy dwelling.
God sets the lonely in families,
>   he leads out the prisoners with singing.

The families we grew up in, whether exemplary or heart-breaking or somewhere in between, are not our *first* family. When we are born again we are born into a new family, utterly unique in this world and the only family enduring forever in the next. We are children of the heavenly Father, brothers and sisters of Christ. That makes them our first family.

It was a great relief and motivator to me when I realized that as a pastor I was not called primarily to be a project manager, a goal-getter, and a strategist. I admire those who can do those things but I'm called to work with the Father to create an environment of a healthy home for God's people.

Many, if not most, churches have features of home without ever thinking too much about it. It is natural for God's household to exhibit the traits of a family. But I have been surprised that what should be so natural has required considerable rethinking on my part (and maybe on yours). I'm reluctant to put it this way, given how this all started, but I'm still learning how our church can *align* with this *vision* of church as home and how I, as a pastor, can be a homemaker.

In our congregation there is one compliment we especially love. It's when someone new says, "When I came here, I felt like I was home."

To consider:

What details define your congregation's environment? Does your worship time define you, or is it your teaching? Are you characterized by your ministries beyond the church or your intimate sense of fellowship? Are there common strands through your main influences?

How does your congregational environment shape your ministries?

2

Ruth: The Love
That Will Not Let Us Go

When I was struggling to find an Old Testament example of God's family, our friend, Dr. Lawson Younger, exclaimed, "What about Ruth?!" (He should know. He's written a fine commentary on the book.) There in this little jewel of a story I found these three disparate people who made up a family of God—Naomi, an embittered prodigal daughter, Ruth, an orphan from a wicked people, and Boaz, the noble, graying bachelor farmer with a keen sense of covenant responsibility. It's a strange way to start a family, but that's how God does things. Your church isn't so different from that.

Ten years had passed since the neighbors stood silent and hungry as the family of four trudged out of Bethlehem with all they owned on their backs. This was in the days of Israel's judges when everyone did what was right in their own eyes and the LORD let them taste the famine of their willful hearts. He forbade the rains to come. Precious seeds never sprouted from the dust. Bethlehem—"House of Bread"—belied its name. Elimelek, the father, heard there was food in Moab, southeast across the Salt Sea, so he abandoned his God-given, God-famished land to put roots down where Moab's blood-thirsty god, Chemosh, reigned, and they went from the frying pan into the fire. Instead of saving his family, he was destroying them. All three men in the family died in Moab, leaving all three wives childless and widowed in a godforsaken land.

Naomi had no reserves of strength or faith. All that was left for her was to return to Bethlehem. Her daughters-in-law weren't sure whether their home was Moab or Judah, so they went with her. Naomi eventually persuaded Orpah to return to Moab, but Ruth refused. Her refusal carried the language of conversion, "Your people will be my people and your God my God" (Ruth 1:16). Naomi had left her people, lost her husband and sons, and her grief had calcified into bitterness against her God, so the two of them were a strange spiritual pair.

The crisis that lay beneath the surface of this story was the impending loss of the family land and line, a matter of far greater consequence to a household in Israel that it would be to us. In Moab, the family of Elimelek

The two of them were a strange spiritual pair.

had teetered on the knife-edge of extinction, for in Israel when a man's family line died out, it was as if he and his ancestors had never existed at all. By the time the two childless, landless survivors returned to Bethlehem, extinction was only a matter of time.[1]

Hungry and Empty

That, believe it or not, is our family story. "Once you were not a people," said Peter (1 Peter 2:10). Like Naomi, or like Israel after their exile, or like the prodigal son, the LORD often brings us home hungry and empty. Naomi's story is an Old Testament version of the prodigal son story.

Perhaps Naomi had no choice but to leave Bethlehem with her husband but when she returned she was wrapped in a shroud of bitterness and defeat. "Don't call me Naomi [Pleasant]," she told the women of Bethlehem when they came out to greet her. "Call me Mara, because the Almighty has made my life very bitter. I went away full, but the LORD has brought me back empty. Why call me Naomi? The LORD has afflicted me; the Almighty has brought misfortune upon me"(Ruth 1:20–21). She was, it seemed to her, as good as dead.

The book of Ruth, on the other hand, is an adoption story. Ruth came to Israel as a spiritual orphan. While she surely wanted Naomi's people to be her people and Naomi's God to be her God, she couldn't make that happen without the welcome of God. No one, after all, can arrange their own adoption. No one can save themselves. But God had undoubtedly taken the initiative in quiet ways even while Ruth was still in Moab.

If there was one moment that established Ruth's adoption into Israel, it must have been when, on that first day of gleaning, Boaz said to her, "I've been told all about what you have done for your mother-in-law since the death of your husband—how you left your father and mother and your homeland and came to live with a people you did not know before. May the LORD repay you for what you have done. May you be richly rewarded by the LORD, the God of Israel, under whose wings you have come to take refuge" (Ruth 2:11–12).

"It's Going to Be the Best Day of My Life"

Let's pause Ruth for a moment for another adoption story. Our friends Doug and Jamie have four little girls, three of them adopted. Recently, Jacqueline, age ten, who is deaf, celebrated her longawaited official day. Jamie made a sash for her to wear that read, "Today is my Adoption Day!" As the family prepared to leave for the courthouse, Jackie signed, "It's going to be the best day of my life."

Jamie said, "I think most of us started weeping at the part where the judge asked her if she understood what adoption was. She signed, 'I know they love me forever, and I will get a new name, and they will adopt me as their daughter always.'" She kept clicking the heels of her fancy shoes and signing, "There's no place like home. There's no place like home."

Out beyond the front yard of God's family, people live restless, unguarded, insecure lives. They are the refugees of Babel, orphaned and landless. They can pursue every pleasure or purpose under the sun but in the end it all adds up to nothing, just so much smoke. The light of the God-blessed life never shines upon them. But those orphans who leave the hopeless behind are guaranteed a home under the refuge of God's wings.

Jamie told me that Jacqueline was born into a terrible situation. She did not trust men and had a hard time trusting Jamie's husband, Doug. Eventually, responding to Jamie's pleas and assurances, she "gave Doug a chance" and began calling him

Daddy. She bought him this plaque for his office: "Any man can be a Father but it takes someone special to be a Daddy."

The Kindness of Boaz

Then there is Boaz. To Ruth that first day, he was a most generous landowner to allow her to follow behind the harvesters and glean the wheat they dropped, but when she came home to Naomi she got a surprise. With a glint in her eye that must have mystified Ruth, Naomi said, "The LORD bless him! . . . He has not stopped showing his kindness to the living and the dead." By "he" Naomi surely meant the LORD. She added, "That man is our close relative; he is one of our guardian-redeemers" (Ruth 2:20). Do you see her sudden change of heart from "the Almighty has brought misfortune upon me"? You can almost see the writer wink.

No other culture established the function of the guardian-redeemer, a male next-of-kin designated to redeem an Israelite's God-given land to original clan ownership. The principle extended to marriage. If a married man died without children, his kinsman-redeemer could and should marry his widow. A child from that marriage would keep the dead man's line alive. He would not be forgotten. His family identity would not be expunged. All this was in order to keep intact the family of God in the land he had given them. But there was a price. If land was redeemed, it was at the kinsman's expense. And if a son was born, he was regarded, not as the kinsman's son and heir, but the son of the man whose name he redeemed. A kinsman-redeemer bore the pricey obligations of redemption.

When Ruth came to the threshing floor and proposed to Boaz one night, it wasn't pure romance. She was appealing to his sense of responsibility as their kinsman-redeemer. The love she hoped for, first and foremost, was Boaz's love of the LORD and His people. It was God's wonderful kindness that Boaz's deep sense of responsibility was entwined with love for Ruth.

By welcoming his responsibility to Naomi and Ruth, Boaz foreshadowed Jesus Himself. Hebrews 2:11 says, "Both the one who makes people holy and those who are made holy are of the same family. So Jesus is not ashamed to call them brothers and sisters." According to Isaiah, the Messiah says, "Here am I, and the children the LORD has given me." Hebrews 2 explains in verses 17–18, "[H]e had to be made like them, fully human in every way, in order that he might become a merciful and faithful high priest in service to God, and that he might make atonement for the sins of the people." In other words, He redeemed us.

Of course, there is one other important character—baby Obed, the miracle child of a once childless woman and an old man. (Does that remind you of anyone else?) When Boaz announced his intention to marry Ruth, one of the elders at the gate said, "May the LORD make the woman who is coming into your home like Rachel and Leah, who together built up the family of Israel," to which everyone shouted *mazel tov*! (Ruth 4:11).

To Naomi, Obed was more than a grandson. When the Women's Choir of Bethlehem gathered around her a year later they sang, "Praise be to the LORD, who this day has not left you without a guardian-redeemer. May he become famous throughout Israel! He will renew your life and sustain you in your old age. For your daughter-in-law, who loves you and who is better to you than seven sons, has given him birth" (Ruth 4:14–15). And when Naomi took the little boy in her arms and cared for him, the women living there said of Naomi (who had come back empty), "Naomi has a son!" (Ruth 4:17).

Finally, the writer tells us that Obed became the grandfather of David, and we know that means he was the forebear of Jesus Christ Himself! What an extraordinary family God made!

The Book of *Hesed*

The most important word in the book of Ruth is *hesed*, translated "kindness." Naomi said to her weeping daughters-in-law, "May the LORD show you *kindness*, as you have shown *kindness* to your dead husbands and to me" (Ruth 1:8). On the evening of that first day of gleaning, when Naomi discovered Ruth's benefactor was Boaz, she said, "The LORD bless him! He [the LORD] has not stopped showing his *kindness* to the living and the dead" (Ruth 2:20). The word appears again in Ruth 3:10 when Boaz tells Ruth that night at the threshing floor, "The LORD bless you, my daughter. This *kindness* is greater than that which you showed earlier: You have not run after the younger men, whether rich or poor."

We don't have an English word big enough for this Hebrew word *hesed*. To do it justice in English we'd need to make a long, run-together compound word: covenant-loyalty-faithful-ness-kindness-goodness-mercy-love-compassion.[2] Even when the word doesn't appear, it is embroidered all through this story. It is such an important word that we could rename Ruth's story *The Book of Hesed: The Love That Will Not Let Us Go*.

Hesed binds God to His people and His people to one another in loyal love. One example is Psalm 118:1. In the familiar Old Testament refrain, "Give thanks to the LORD, for he is good; his *love* endures forever," that word is *hesed*. It is the very definition of God's love for His people, used dozens of times of God. Paul, who thought in Hebrew even when he wrote in Greek, surely had *hesed* in mind when he wrote to the Romans, "I am convinced that neither death nor life, neither angels nor demons, neither the present nor the future, nor any powers, neither height nor depth, nor anything else in all creation, will be able to separate us from *the love of God* that is in Christ Jesus our Lord" (Rom. 8:38–39).

Ruth's story taught the people of Israel, as it teaches us, that *hesed*-love was to be the distinguishing quality of our relationships. Believers cannot really know or obey God without bringing this kind of love to each other. Nothing less will do. In the New Testament Paul set out to define the love we are to have for one another in 1 Corinthians 13.

> Love is patient, love is kind. It does not envy, it does not boast, it is not proud. It does not dishonor others, it is not self-seeking, it is not easily angered, it keeps no record of wrongs. Love does not delight in evil but rejoices with the truth. It always protects, always trusts, always hopes, always perseveres.

That is *hesed*. No matter what other spiritual wonders or sacrifices we bring to church in our hip pocket, without this kind of love exercised within our church family, we have nothing to offer. A church family is intended by God to be bound by loyal, long-suffering *hesed* love. This is love that rises from our new covenant through Christ and embraces all our Christian kin.

Your church family undoubtedly includes people who feel homeless or who are en route from *Bitter* back to *Pleasant* through a valley heavy with the dark silence of God. But among us are also those like Boaz, noble men and women who spread the blessing of God like wings over His people. We also all have the capacity to spread God's wings of refuge over others through prayer.

A church family is intended by God to be bound by loyal, long-suffering *hesed* love.

By contrast, the unnamed and now-forgotten first kinsman was unwilling to "endanger my own estate" in order to preserve the land and line of Elimelek, as God expected him to do. He was only interested in the land. Since he refused his duty to "maintain the name of the dead," *his* name is forgotten. To have his name expunged was his punishment, a way of saying to all the generations to follow that those who will not fulfill their obligations within the family of God are soon forgotten.

Jesus: How We Are to Love

In John 13:34–35 Jesus spells out three distinctives of our love for one another.

- "A new command I give you: Love one another." To love one another is the new and defining command of the church. Failure sounds like a cymbal dropped on a tile floor. There is no substitute.

- "As I have loved you, so you must love one another." Jesus' love for us is the measure we must use to evaluate our love for others. Thus our love must be sacrificial, servant-hearted, and full of grace.

- "By this everyone will know that you are my disciples, if you love one another." The foolproof evidence of our devotion to Christ is our love for our Christian brothers and sisters. Our worship services are not nearly such a clear statement of our love of Christ as is our love for one another.

So why does so little of our strategic planning go to assuring a deep Christlike love for one another? Why do we often put so much more effort to establishing our budget than investing in our love for our brothers and sisters? Lawson Younger says, "The very idea of 'doing hesed' does not cross the minds of many a church attendee who is more interested in having his or her own needs met."[3]

I have watched a single, older woman in our church, living on a small fixed income, take under her wing a single mom and her four kids. She's chauffeured them, fed them, babysat them, had us all praying for them, raised funds for car repair, and has brought them to church. She has become a surrogate grandmother and a kind of modern-day kinsman-redeemer.

I had a friend many years ago who was admitted to a psych ward with severe depression. She asked if I'd come to her support group as a surrogate family member. Each patient introduced their supporter to the others. One woman, whose depression hung on her like a heavy black coat, introduced her friend in such a way that I knew they were both Christians and that they'd been friends for a long time. I remember thinking how hard it must have been for that friend to be faithful and safe for her suffering sister over the months and years. Our love for one another in the church family isn't always easy. But that is *hesed*. That is loyal love.

To consider:

Who in your congregation exemplifies *hesed* love, and what is the effect on the church?

How might your church leaders strengthen the congregation's sense of covenant bonds with one another?

3

Brothers and Sisters

As a child in California in the 1970s, Jeff wondered who he was. "I never looked like anybody growing up," he said. "Everybody looked like somebody, but I was the odd man out." Finally, a few years ago he and his brother took a DNA test and, sure enough, they didn't have the same father.

As it happened, a couple of years later a woman named Julie, an amateur genealogist, was trying to learn more about her roots and had her DNA analyzed. There were no matches with anyone in the genealogy company's database so she put the whole business aside. Some months later, she checked the database again and this time there was a match. She was apparently closely related to a guy who'd also had his DNA tested. She looked at his photo and remembers thinking, "He looked exactly like my father." She sent the man an email and five minutes later she had Jeff's reply.

The DNA database also showed that Jeff had another unknown sister, Beth, whose birth father was the same as his. The three of them arranged a reunion. Julie remembers, "It is kind of weird finding a brother when you're in your fifties and he's just a dead ringer for our father—the way he walks and his laugh and some of the expressions on his face."

More time passed. A San Diego man, Brandon, who knew he'd been adopted, decided to get a DNA test, too. Lo and behold, he also matched Jeff as well as Julie and Beth. "'It's really wonderful,' [Brandon] said of rediscovering his birth family. 'My adoptive parents had passed on, my adoptive brother had passed on. I thought I was a party of one and now I'm a party of 110.'"[1]

That's our kind of story.

The Brother from Madagascar and Other Kin

What is it that can bind four perfect strangers together like that? They didn't just want to meet for curiosity's sake. They wanted to be together, to be the family they had never been before.

I've seen the same phenomenon among Christians. I heard the couple in the booth behind us at a restaurant visiting with the waitress, asking her all about her life. Then I heard the woman ask the waitress, "Could I pray for you?" and I knew I had spiritual kin in that booth.

A few years ago my wife and I attended a small international church in Limassol, Cyprus. Among the congregation were several Filipino domestic workers who led the singing, a couple who were refugees from Syria, about twenty Cypriots, and four pastors! The pastor of the church was of Indian background and British citizenship. A visiting missionary was from Ireland. A French navy chaplain, who spoke no English, was from Madagascar. And then there was me. We all took pictures together. Brothers and sisters who'd never met and yet were kin in Christ.

How is that possible? Paul explained to the Ephesians how they had been bound together with Jewish believers, despite "the dividing wall of hostility" that long guarded the Jews from Gentiles. Christ Jesus, said Paul, "has made the two groups one.... His purpose was to create in himself one new humanity out of the two.... Consequently, you are no longer foreigners and strangers, but fellow citizens with God's people and members of his household" (Eph. 2:14–19). I remember looking at that brother from Madagascar. He was small and dark and didn't understand a word we were saying; yet we each knew that we shared Christ. Somewhere he had learned the gospel as I had. He sang and prayed as I do. He treasured the same Scriptures that I treasure, and holds citizenship in the same kingdom as I.

Our First Family

Those four reunited siblings shared family resemblances. Among Christians our distinguishing family feature is this: "By this everyone will know that you are my disciples, if you love one another" (John 13:15).

Christians are referred to as brothers 139 times in the New Testament. (Some Bible translations translate the Greek *adelphoi* as *brothers* because it is a masculine form, but it is clear in most cases that both men and women are being addressed, whether or not the translation expresses both.) Regarding one another as brothers and sisters was far more radical than we realize. In our culture, we're used to speaking of people outside our family as brothers and sisters. A "band of brothers" describes a tight-knit military unit. Sometimes athletic teams will use the terms, as do good friends. But that almost *never* happened in the language of New Testament times. No one called someone a brother or sister who wasn't a blood relative. In fact, the entire perspective on family in that culture was dramatically different from ours.

In his book, *When the Church Was a Family*, Joseph Hellerman explains three principles:

Principle #1: "In the New Testament world the group took priority over the individual."

Principle #2: "In the New Testament world a person's most important group was his blood family."

Principle #3: "In the New Testament world the closest family bond was not the bond of marriage. It was the bond between siblings."

Hellerman concludes, "I trust that you are beginning to see why we cannot simply import our American idea of what it means to be a brother or sister into our interpretation of the New Testament. 'Brother' meant immeasurably more to the strong-group authors of the Bible than the word means to you and me—it was their most important family relationship. At this point you are now prepared, perhaps for the first time ever, to properly appreciate what the early Christians meant when they referred to one another as brothers and sisters in Christ."[2]

Maybe you should read that last paragraph again to be sure it registered.

Likewise, there is the startling New Testament usage of the Greek word *philadelphian,* as in 2 Peter 1:7 where believers are admonished to add to their "godliness, *mutual affection*; and to mutual affection, love." *Philadelphian* is also translated *brotherly love.* In their commentary on 2 Peter and Jude, Dick Lucas and Christopher Green wrote, "The New Testament is the only place where the word has been found outside the context of a home. A first-century reader would therefore come across it here with a sense of shock; Peter really does mean that Christians should have a quality of relationships which is demonstrably different and satisfying, demanding a high and new loyalty."[3]

So with that in mind, try to wrap your head around how radical it was when Jesus said this in Mark 3:31–35:

> Then Jesus' mother and brothers arrived. Standing outside, they sent someone in to call him. A crowd was sitting around him, and they told him, "Your mother and brothers are outside looking for you."
>
> "Who are my mother and my brothers?" he asked.
>
> Then he looked at those seated in a circle around him and said, "Here are my mother and my brothers! Whoever does God's will is my brother and sister and mother."

Once, according to Mark 10:28–30, Peter said to Jesus, "We have left everything to follow you!" To which Jesus replied, "Truly I tell you, no one who has left home or brothers or sisters or mother or father or children or fields for me and the gospel will fail to receive a hundred times as much in this present age: homes, brothers, sisters, mothers, children and fields—along with persecutions—and in the age to come eternal life."

A brother in our congregation who is from a Muslim-dominated country described the threats on his life when he became a Christian. Among other things, his uncle pressed a knife to his side, demanding he turn away from his faith in Christ. Our brother told us, "Before Christ I didn't like my family. But when I saw Christ and Christ transformed my heart, Christ give me big love for my family, for my parents. I was really a good son. I obeyed my parents and I love them with Jesus' love, but even though I loved them they hated me . . . I love my family, my brother and sisters, but they beat me, they hate me and it was hard to understand. I said, 'Oh God, I am losing one valuable thing—my family—and it was very hard to understand.' But God said, 'I will give you a new family.'"

> **"I said, 'Oh God, I am losing my family.' But God said, 'I will give you a new family.'"**

This is not only true for those rejected by their blood relatives, but for all believers. If you're a Christian, your first family is your fellow believers—those who "do God's will." Let that sink in. *Your Christian brothers and sisters are your first family in Christ.*

Where Does That Leave My Spouse and Kids?

Thinking of the church as our *first family* sounds dangerous because we all know how families have suffered, sometimes irreparably, from neglect in the name of church. Some pastors go whole weeks without a night at home. Too many Christians have hidden at church from their family responsibilities at home. Scripture certainly does not advocate that!

The Bible tells us how to have strong marriages and families, how to honor our parents, and how to care for our extended families. The pastoral epistles of 1 Timothy and Titus give qualifications for elders that include the wise and proper care of their families. In fact, our homes are a sort of seminary preparing us for church leadership. (More on that in chapter 11.) Paul teaches us the demanding commitments of submission and love in marriage and parenting. Seeing God's people as our first family must never be an excuse to neglect our spouse and kids.

That said—and said strongly—I've seen too many Christian families who are not anchored in the relationships of God's first family, the church. Christians are raising children who, like them, see church as an event, not a family; who see being with God's people as an optional weekend activity. They skip church for all manner of activities, and do not regularly connect their families with others in the congregation.

Some children's and youth ministries have virtually no link to the rest of the church body, leaving the kids with no sense of being in a big family with other believers. Is it any wonder that Barna Group research shows that "Millennials are leaving the church. Nearly six in ten (59%) young people who grow up in Christian churches end up walking away, and the unchurched segment among Millennials has increased in the last decade from 44% to 52%, mirroring a larger cultural trend away from churchgoing in America. When asked what has helped their faith grow, 'church' does not make even the top 10 factors."[4]

Good news comes in another Barna article quoting a study

by David Kinnaman: "Those [Millenials] who stay were twice as likely to have a close personal friendship with an adult inside the church. . . . This stands true from the inverse angle as well: Seven out of 10 Millennials who dropped out of church did not have a close friendship with an adult and nearly nine out of ten never had a mentor at the church."[5]

We all know the dangers of parents who spend too little time with their kids, but what of the dangers of Christian kids and their parents who have no sense that our Lord Jesus expects them deeply engaged in loving relationships with other believers? Remember, Jesus said there are no marriage bonds in heaven, only the bonds of God's people with one another and the Lord.

Our church friends, Kelvin and Anne Tohme, live and serve on a Christian university campus near us. Along with their two children, Landon (ten) and Lauryn (eight), they live in a small two-bedroom campus apartment. Anne is a gifted communicator and was one of the people I asked to speak to our congregation about the church as our first family. She said,

> In our family there are often times when Kelvin or I are gone because of our campus duties and ministries. When we talk with our kids about this—about why mom or dad are gone—we explain to them that it's because we are a part of two families. We have our family of the four of us, but we are also part of a bigger family—the family of God—and we have a role in both families and we need to care for both families. And yes, we may miss that person when they are gone, but we know how important it is that they go. Ultimately, our role as parents and the church is to raise up our children to advance the kingdom—shouldn't they see us modeling that? Shouldn't they see us (and participate

with us) in loving the family of God and not just our own little family?

Anne tells about a season when their young son, Landon, was going through a rough time at school. "One day, we were just walking along and he says to me, 'Mom, my safe places are home and at church.' Well, you can imagine as a mother what that did to me, but that told me something that Landon didn't even know how to articulate. He knew that at home and with the people of God he was loved. He knew that he was a part of two families."

Anne told me they relate to the example of Ryan Kwon, who pastors Resonate Church in Fremont, California. He uses the phrase "family win."

Ryan, the son of Korean immigrants, described how his well-educated father "worked a maintenance job cleaning bathrooms at LAX Airport. Why? For the family win—so that his kids could have a better education and, ultimately, a better life than if he had stayed in Korea. Even as a child, however, Ryan was also expected to make sacrifices for his family, because 'if the family didn't win, no one won.'"[6]

As a Christian, a family win brings an advantage to our heavenly Father and our brothers and sisters in Christ. That's what Ryan means when he says, "Learn to fight not only for your first name, but for your last name." So Anne says, "Our first name: Tohme. Our last name: Christian."

My dear friend, Bill, grew up as an only child of non-Christian parents in a rather cold home in Boston. When he was about eight, two women, one who worked with Bill's mom at a factory, came around the neighborhood, inviting kids to a new Sunday school they were starting in Bill's elementary school building. So Bill went and kept going. Sometimes one of the women would invite him to dinner. When the weather was bad, one of them picked him up. Often they would invite Bill home for Sunday dinner with their families. When he was fourteen Bill accepted Christ at Bible camp. As the Sunday school kids got older, these women took them to special events like youth rallies and to the symphony in Boston. Bill says, "It was like having a bunch of brothers and sisters."

That's exactly what it's like. I've realized that it rattles people a little to tell them their church is their first family. They're afraid I'm downplaying our responsibilities at home. But it is just the opposite. A healthy church home is God's gift to any family. When our son was very young we lived more than a thousand miles from his only grandparent and we were seldom able to make that trip. So we asked the Holts if they'd be substitute grandparents for him, a task they embraced wholeheartedly. A church is a big family of grandparents, parents, brothers, and sisters, all working with Jesus to make each and all of us more like Him.

To consider:

Can you restate (for memory's sake) the significance of the New Testament calling Christians "brothers and sisters"?

How would your church change if people thought of it as their "first family"?

4

Love's Coat
of Many Colors

Galatians 6:10 says, "Therefore, as we have opportunity, let us do good to all people, especially to those who belong to the family of believers." In his commentary on that verse, the church father, Jerome, around AD 400, told a story that had been handed down to him.

> The blessed John the Evangelist lived in Ephesus until extreme old age. His disciples could barely carry him to church and he could not muster the voice to speak many words. During individual gatherings he usually said nothing but, "Little children, love one another." The disciples and brothers in attendance, annoyed because they always heard the same words, finally said, "Teacher, why do you always say this?" He replied with a line worthy of John: "Because it is the Lord's commandment and if it alone is kept, it is sufficient."[1]

The Lord's commandment appears three times in John 13:34–35 (plus once in Romans, twice in 1 Peter, and six times in 1 and 2 John): "A new command I give you: *Love one another*. As I have loved you, so *you must love one another*. By this everyone will know that you are my disciples, *if you love one another*." Nothing else shows the world around us such clear evidence of regeneration and of God's infusion of transforming grace as the radical realignment of our relationships in Christ as seen in the family of God, the local church.

But What Does Christian Love Look Like?

Loving one another takes some doing. I was looking at a photo on Facebook of two brothers, ages ten and six, gingerly holding their brand-new baby brother. Big toothy grins, wide eyes, excited beyond measure, still trying to wrap their heads around this wonder. But guess what? I predict they won't always be so affectionate! There will be days when they aren't so glad to be brothers.

Church is like that. I have loved church people and been loved by them all my life. I love the rural church I grew up in and I've loved the congregations I've served. But I also used to get a stomachache before every congregational meeting because I was afraid of getting bushwhacked by critical comments. And it wasn't so long ago when my chairman came to tell me how unkind I'd been in an Elder Board meeting and insisted I apologize (pretty much like my mom used to do). Then, truth be told, I've had times when I just didn't want to be around the church folks. But in all these times, we're still family.

Loving other believers is in our spiritual DNA, a kind of gene therapy accomplished by the Holy Spirit. First John 5:1 says, "Everyone who believes that Jesus is the Christ is born of God, and everyone who loves the father *loves his child as well."* Our love for one another is not exactly like other kinds of love. Coming from Christ as it does, our love now is capable of extraordinary sacrifice as well as redemptive effects—not to save from sin, of course, but to rescue and restore our brothers and sisters in other ways. Our love can be divinely wise and infused with God's own truth, so that we know not only how to love *much* but to love *well*. Perhaps most astonishing, our Christlike love comes with the makings of a servant nature.

Serve One Another Humbly

Several art prints hang in our church. I call it the quiet disciple-ship of art. One of them is Ford Madox Brown's painting, "Jesus Washing Peter's Feet." (Go ahead, look it up.) Jesus is drying Peter's foot, while Peter looks down embarrassed and speech-less. The other apostles in the background are looking intently over the table at what Jesus is doing. One has his chin buried in his fists on the table, hair hanging into his eyes. There's a small bag of coins near his arm. At the near end of the table, another leans low as if to get a better look while he loosens his own sandals. Another holds his head in his hands, fingers splayed, shocked. John looks over Peter's shoulder, mouth agape.

We talk so easily about "Christian service" that we may not realize what makes *Christian* service so shocking. It isn't *what* we do. It's the *attitude*. Jesus said in Matthew 23:8–12,

> "But you are not to be called 'Rabbi,' for you have one Teacher, and you are all *brothers*. And do not call anyone on earth 'father,' for you have one Father, and he is in heaven. Nor are you to be called instructors, for you have one Instructor, the Messiah. *The*

> *greatest among you will be your servant.* For those who exalt
> themselves will be humbled, and those who humble themselves
> will be exalted."

Christian service strips away our titles and ranks because
we are all servant siblings, like a family of maids and butlers.

It's not enough to think of ourselves as equals. In Philippians
2:3–4, Paul told believers, "In humility value others *above your-selves*, not looking to your own interests but each of you to the
interests of the others. In your relationships with one another,
have the same mindset as Christ Jesus." You might say it goes
downhill from there because Jesus, according to verse 7, "made
himself nothing by taking the very nature of a servant."

Have you noticed how a waiter will say, "Hi, I'm Jack, and
I'll be your *server* tonight." Never *servant.* That would be too
demeaning. None of us are naturally eager for the title of
servant. Except for Jesus. He was a servant at heart, humble
enough in serving that He became "obedient to death—even
death on a cross" (Phil. 2:8).

That's the rub when it comes to Christian service—that
self-sacrificing humility. It isn't the task that is the test. It's
doing it with the very *nature* of a servant. Often, people like
to serve at church. They *like* to sing, or teach, or manage the
finances. But let someone actually treat us like a servant and
the claws come out.

Our previous church had a rather sprawling building. My
pet peeve was that on Sundays, after everyone left, it was no
one's job to be sure all the doors were locked. I'd been stand-ing for hours. My feet and back hurt. I was hungry. *Surely*
there was someone besides me who could check all those
the doors. After all, I was the Senior Pastor. But whenever I

decided to raise the subject, I could almost hear the Lord say, "Would it kill you to do one thing in church that no one sees, one thing that's 'below' your rank? Keep it to yourself."

A few months ago I learned that a small group of young adults from our church had gone to help one of our shut-ins with cleaning and encouragement. They were at it for two or three days! It was servant work. Even though almost no one saw it, they made our family stronger.

Christian service begins within our church home. The myriad ways we serve our brothers and sisters in Christ—some of which we'll look at in the chapters to come—have no parallel anywhere else if done with the Christlike nature of a servant.

Years ago, when I was preaching on the story of Jesus' washing the disciples' feet, we arranged for our Associate Pastor to wash the feet of one of our church leaders, Harold, while a soloist sang Michael Card's "The Basin and the Towel." It all went off without a hitch. I preached my sermon and was just ready to have people stand for the benediction when Harold spoke up from the back of the church, "Can I say something?" "Uh, okay," I said nervously. Harold walked to the front. He faced the folks, all choked up. "I just want to say, that was the most incredible thing—having my feet washed like that. I'm just overwhelmed by it." That was it. That's what is liable to happen when Jesus' people serve one another as He served us.

Elusive Authenticity

I get suspicious when I look at a church website and see stock photos of smiling, perfect people, taken in perfect light, a picture I know wasn't taken in that church. It's just too perfect.

With just a little effort we can make ourselves look better than we are. But that is a deadly endeavor, especially in the pursuit of church growth.

I confess I wonder what else in that congregation isn't genuine. I realize I'm not being fair, but I wonder what they're trying to prove.

The trouble with authenticity in a church is that it's not always very impressive. With just a little effort we can make ourselves look better than we are. Not more authentic, just better-looking. But that is a deadly endeavor, especially in the pursuit of church growth. Paul wrote in Romans 12:9, "Love must be sincere," i.e., genuine, not hypocritical, not theatrical.

I'm not sure we're doing anyone a favor only putting our best people forward in worship when we have other capable people who would so love to have a part. I'm not suggesting we use people who are incompetent or unprepared. Yet love for one another and for our guests involves a certain degree of vulnerability and authenticity on our part. When we use a cross-section of our congregation in worship, we and our guests see us as we are. In my home church out in the country when I was growing up, each family took turns being responsible for that Sunday's "special music." It wasn't always pretty, but it was who we were. I don't think that would fly now, but that's what I mean by congregational vulnerability. That's where love comes in.

We've adopted a phrase in our church: "We will paint with the colors God gives us." That means we will try to use as many of our people as we can in order to portray the Lord and His blessings in worship services and other ministries of our church. We don't structure our services to appeal to a certain kind of audience. We don't always use our best musicians. Our styles of music shift, depending on who is on board on a given Sunday morning.[2] Not everyone agrees with me, of course, but I think of this practice as being authentic, as if to say, "This is who we are before God. This is our family at worship."

Gerardo Marti has written a book examining how worship music works in multiracial congregations. He studied how twelve successfully integrated churches approached music. You might think that their music reflected all their different cultures but what Marti discovered was . . . well . . . it didn't really matter. Michael O. Emerson, who reviewed the book for *Christianity Today*, wrote:

> [Marti] asks you to imagine your child, niece, or nephew doing a musical solo—perhaps it is at a school recital, or perhaps in your church's children's choir.
>
> What do the adults do? No matter what the music, no matter how well or poorly performed, they cheer, usually while standing, and usually filled with a mixture of joy and pride. The point is not whether the children "did well." The point is that they are our children, and we are proud of them for being up there, representing us.
>
> This is exactly the answer Marti arrives at through his extensive analysis of what is actually occurring in multiracial congregations, and through his insightful interviews with parishioners, choir members, and church leaders.
>
> What "succeeds" musically in multiracial churches is not a certain type of music or how well it is performed. Rather, it is: (a) people of various backgrounds all practicing together, spending time together, singing together, worshiping together; and (b) the fact that it is "our choir, our people."[3]

My point here, of course, is that's true in all kinds of churches because God made us to function as a family.

I was talking with a young man from another city who began to tell me about a large church there with great musicians. He is a musician and knows many of these people. He was particularly acquainted with their youth ministry and he was troubled by what he saw. Everything was so polished, so exciting, so show business, that he suspected most of those teenagers would drop out of church when they graduated. "Because it just isn't authentic," he said. "It doesn't represent the church as they are or as God made them to be."

Our Christian love comes out in authenticity. I heard a story a long time ago about a small church where a guy got up to sing a solo. Right from the start he couldn't find his pitch, even with the piano banging out the tune. But as he stumbled along, people started grabbing hymnals (remember those?), and looking up the page of the song he was singing. By the second verse, they were joining in, and by the third verse, they had become a choir. Then, as if on cue, they all stopped and let the fellow sing the last verse on his own and on pitch. I'd have loved to be in that service!

On the Agenda

As church leaders, we are entrusted with overseeing our church family's love for one another. Like parents, we are entrusted with cultivating family unity and love. Think of the things parents do to strengthen their families: insisting on certain meals together, family fun times like game or movie nights, family celebrations, shared chores, reinforced respect

("That is no way to treat your brother!"), a sense of family heritage ("Remember who you are."), and loyalty ("You take care of your sister. She looks up to you."). Church leaders can adapt virtually the same strategies to develop our church-family relationships.

Most churches foster loving relationships, even when we haven't thought much about it. But my experience is that church leaders are likely to invest far more thought and time in strategies for numerical growth than in strategies for building strong church-family bonds. The Bible never tells us to grow our churches bigger

It is much easier to count noses than to measure love.

but it tells us again and again to love one another (which must be an indication that it isn't so easy as it might sound). Still, it's much easier to count noses than to measure love. We too easily take our relationships for granted . . . until the wheels come off. Regular oversight of our relationships must be on the leadership agenda.

Psalm 133:1 says, "How good and pleasant it is when God's people dwell together in unity." *The Message* puts it, "How wonderful, how beautiful, when brothers and sisters get along!"

But it doesn't always happen.

Sibling Rivalry

Esther (Eppie) and Pauline Friedman were identical twins born on July 4, 1918. At age twenty-one they were married to their husbands in a double wedding. In 1955 Eppie took over an advice column in the *Chicago Sun-Times* called "Ask Ann Landers." Only a few months later Pauline took up a similar column, "Dear Abby," under the name Abigail Van Buren. Trouble began when Pauline offered their hometown paper, the *Sioux City Journal*, a lower rate for her "Dear Abby" column if the paper promised not to print her sister's "Ask Ann Landers." Eppie was furious. They both became very successful advice columnists, but their relationship was never the same. They counseled people on *relationships*, for crying out loud! Even after they both died, their children continued to feud.[4]

It comes as no surprise to anyone that some church families feud similarly. Believers are not exempt from sibling rivalry. Take Paul's poignant plea in Philippians 4:2–3, "I plead with Euodia and I plead with Syntyche to be of the same mind in the Lord. Yes, and I ask you, my true companion, help these women since they have contended at my side in the cause of the gospel." Here were two esteemed Christian sisters who had a reputation for contending for the gospel but had become merely contentious. Their conflict had become so serious that word reached Paul. It's interesting that he didn't just adjudicate the matter. "Euodia, give it up. Syntyche is right. Case closed!" That wasn't his approach.

I learned in a management seminar about the binary trap, which is when it seems that a problem can only have either a 0 or a 1 kind of solution. One or the other. Either Euodia is right or Syntyche is. It's a trap because often there are other ways of coming at an issue. Paul pleads for a third option: "be of the same mind in the Lord." That doesn't necessarily mean coming to the same conclusion about their issue. How could these two Christian sisters, whose conflict was so deep set, ever be of the same mind?

The church cannot be much of a home unless we learn to

resolve conflicts like these. (Actually, that is why there are so many churches that are such dysfunctional families). Brotherly love—mutual esteem—is tough because so much is required of us to maintain it.

Brotherly love is tough because so much is required of us to maintain it.

When church leaders become aware of a love-damaging conflict within the congregation, we must help as Paul did. I recall a situation that blew up between two people in a thoughtless, unguarded moment. It brewed for a week, so our elders met after a morning service to put our heads together. We prayed and one of our leaders agreed to place phone calls to each party to sort things out and to give biblical encouragement to resolve the matter. Things were dicey for a week or two, but one person was especially gracious, and God smoothed the waters. There was a sweet agreement to forgive and forget.

Some conflicts seem intractable. In fact, some are. But we can take heart knowing that the Holy Spirit is still at work even when brothers and sisters stop loving one another. I remember despairing over warring believers and then remembering that, despite appearances, the Spirit was present in each of them, working clandestinely from the inside out. In times of trouble, our prayers should start with that assurance. We are not helpless. The Spirit helps us in our weaknesses, not only in knowing what to pray, but in the way He works to change in hearts.

Love is always more multifaceted than it seems. Colossians 3:12–14 describes love's coat of many colors. "As God's chosen people, holy and dearly loved, clothe yourselves with compassion, kindness, humility, gentleness and patience. Bear with each other and forgive one another if any of you has a grievance against someone. Forgive as the Lord forgave you. And over all these virtues put on love, which binds them all together in perfect unity."

That is a conflict resolution passage. It's what Euodia and Syntyche needed. They didn't necessarily need to know who was right, but they needed to wash one another's feet with grace. It's the biblical answer to the binary trap. Every virtue listed in Colossians 3—compassion, kindness, humility, gentleness, patience, forbearance, and forgiveness—costs us something. They all come with a basin and towel. They are all undeserved graces, which we give humbly to our sister or brother. And, not coincidentally, they all make us more like Jesus.

"Lord, how many times shall I forgive my brother or sister who sins against me?" Peter asked. "Up to seven times?" Jesus answered, "I tell you, not seven times, but seventy-seven times" (Matt. 18:21–22). Lots and lots of grace.

The Mess I Made

Many years ago I badly offended a woman in my church. I'll call her Debbie. I spoke unkindly to her from my position of power in a congregational meeting. It would have offended anyone, I suppose, but for her it drew a kind of rage. She was a victim of sexual abuse and a male exerting power like I did set off a deep anger and icy distance. It was hard to be in the same church. It was hard sometimes to preach with her glaring at me.

But here's the thing. I didn't go to her. I was afraid. Shortly before we moved from that church, she and her husband came to see me. She did what I should have done. She apologized to me and we patched things up. I've always felt badly about the whole mess.

Over the years, I've followed "Debbie" on Facebook. She would occasionally write a kind comment about something I posted. Not long ago, I decided to write her. Here is our exchange.

Debbie, I often think with great regret how badly I handled my relationship with you for that season at church. I knew so little of the suffering of abuse victims then. And I was so scared of confrontation that I wouldn't go to you to talk it through. I think often—often—of your courage in coming to see me first. I tell that story in my class, as a warning to my students.

I learned a great deal about pastoring from those who have suffered abuse. When I see the smile in your picture, I'm heartened at the grace of God to you . . . and to me.

Lee, thank you so much for sharing your heart. You don't know how much your words mean to me. I have tears running down my face now. I am so sorry for the pain and heartache I caused you during those last months you were here. I so appreciated you helping me to first meet [the counselor] who put me on my pilgrimage to healing. I know I didn't always handle situations right. I wish I could go back and undo the pain I caused people around me. But like you said—through God's grace we move forward.

Debbie, I think the burden of responsibility was on me. Often as I've read your nice comments on my FB page I've been humbled even more. I lived through much of my ministry with a great fear of what I call "the mess," which is what our relationship was for a while. I spent six months in counseling here some years ago, long overdue, because I was so often fearful of who was upset with me—even when they weren't! I do not say this lightly, Debbie: you are a saint, and a gift of God, to your family, your church, and to me.

Lee, I don't know what to say. You have given me a special gift, your friendship. I ask your forgiveness for all the pain I caused you during what you termed "the mess." I know you had a change of spirit/heart. I could sense it in what you shared.

Yes, that's true. The old man has made progress. Though I'm still afraid sometimes of messes. Interestingly my greatest advantage in ministry, especially to other pastors, has been vulnerability. I hear it often. I suspect that is true of you as well.

"Above all, love each other deeply, because love covers over a multitude of sins" (1 Peter 4:8).

The Message captures the sense that love is our spiritual birthright in its paraphrase of 1 John 4:17: "God is love. When we take up permanent residence in a life of love, we live in God and God lives in us. This way, love has the run of the house, becomes at home and mature in us, so that we're free of worry on Judgment Day—our standing in the world is identical with Christ's."

To consider:

Undoubtedly your church has many loving servants. Take a few minutes and identify them in your mind, thanking God for them. Maybe you should write some thank-you notes.

Why do you think church leaders give little time to evaluating how well your church obeys Christ's command to "love one another"?

Philemon: Fresh Starts Refresh Hearts

L ike the book of Ruth, Paul's letter to Philemon is not one of the centerpiece books of the Bible. In fact, it is kind of puzzling why it is even in the Bible. A mere twenty-five verses, the epistle mainly focuses on the apostle's appeal to a wealthy man about his runaway slave. Why is the story relevant to us as we struggle and strive to live as true family? Read on.

Philemon must have just stared, speechless for a moment. Runaway slaves did not return to their masters on their own. But there he was, big as life. Onesimus had stolen away months before, and now he stood in the doorway, holding out two sealed letters. "These are from our brother Paul," he said. "One is for the church and the other is for you." Philemon's surprise doubled. Paul, the venerable apostle of Jesus Christ who was in prison in Rome, had sent him a letter by the hand of his escaped slave . . . who called him *brother*?!

Philemon was a wealthy Christian in whose home the Colossian church met. Paul had never visited Colossae but he knew Philemon well. Paul had probably led him to Christ because he wrote, "You owe me your very self" (v. 19). It's obvious in his letter that Paul loved and admired this brother.

Philemon probably had a number of household slaves. Slavery in that culture wasn't necessarily like the brutal, dehumanizing bondage we think of today. Many slaves were more like indentured servants, living normal lives, and even collecting wages, but they were not free to leave until their term of service was over. So when Onesimus went on the lam, he swindled Philemon out of the debt he owed him. The letter also hints that he might have also stolen money from him before he fled. Onesimus's name meant "useful," but for Philemon, he turned out to be worse than useless.

Onesimus disappeared into the vast Roman Empire, eventually making his way 1,300 miles west to Rome. There he *happened* to meet the apostle Paul, who was a prisoner in chains. (What were the chances?) Not only that, but they figured out that they *both* knew Philemon. In time, Paul brought Onesimus to faith in Christ and they became very close. In his letter, Paul told Philemon that Onesimus "became my son while I was in chains. . . . my very heart" (vv. 10, 12).

Under Paul's tutelage, Onesimus grew in Christian maturity. Eventually, despite his usefulness, they both realized that he needed to return to Philemon. Before Onesimus left, Paul wrote two letters; one to the Colossian church (our book of Colossians) and the other to Philemon personally. Then he dispatched Onesimus, "our faithful and dear brother," along with another "dear brother," Tychicus, to deliver the letters. So imagine Philemon's surprise when he saw these two men—especially Onesimus—on his doorstep!

A Christian Family Story

Where the Old Testament has its *hesed*-driven story of Ruth, the New Testament has Philemon, a little twenty-five-verse vignette of Christian brotherhood.

In his letter to Philemon Paul addressed him as "our dear friend and fellow worker," and also greeted "Apphia our sister" (probably Philemon's wife) and "Archippus our fellow soldier" (perhaps their adult son or one of the church's founders). Paul could not have spoken more highly of Philemon. Look at the priority of loving kinship as Paul reconnects with Philemon in verses 4–7:

> I always thank my God as I remember you in my prayers, because I hear about *your love for all his holy people* and your faith in the Lord Jesus. I pray that your *partnership with us in the faith* may be effective in deepening your understanding of every good thing *we share* for the sake of Christ. *Your love has given me great joy and encouragement, because you, brother, have refreshed the hearts of the Lord's people.*

Isn't it interesting that everything commendable here is relational? Paul thanks God for a leader who loves the other saints in the congregation. He prays that their relationship would draw them into the treasury of all we have in Christ, suggesting that God's best is discovered in partnerships. Philemon's love for fellow believers "refreshed the hearts of the Lord's people," giving them a kind of relational Sabbath.

Recently, a friend told me about a saint in a nearby congregation who died at just shy of her ninety-eighth birthday. My friend wrote, "Elaine was spiritual sweetness embodied. Her soft, positive demeanor was like vitamins and soothing balm bundled together. I rather suspect she was the sort of saint who gives the Church 'silent cement' through her private prayers. Every Saturday morning she would pray through the whole church directory. She declined other plans for that time because prayer was her plan." Her longtime pastor added, "I've never before seen such a strong meekness and such love for me, Christ and His Word." Elaine, like Philemon, "refreshed the hearts of the Lord's people."

The Price of Homecoming

Paul wouldn't have said he was buttering up Philemon, but he was sharpening the point of his letter, which was, to paraphrase, "I appeal to your Christian love. Please take Onesimus back, not as a runaway slave but as a beloved brother in Christ. This once useless slave has become an indispensable Christian servant." In fact, Paul says, "He is very dear to me but even dearer to you, both as a fellow man and as a brother in the Lord."

You have to admit, Paul lays it on pretty thick! But it is all true because this is the kind of change Jesus brings to a life. "I would have liked to keep him with me so that he could take your place in helping me while I am in chains for the gospel. . . . So if you consider me a partner, welcome him as you would welcome me."

The onus was on Philemon. Since the letter was read publicly, everyone was watching what he would do. I wonder if some in that congregation felt he had every right—maybe even a duty—to throw the book at Onesimus, regardless of whether he was a Christian or not. Perhaps others thought some kind of probation was in order. But clearly the apostle Paul wanted Onesimus welcomed into the fellowship with open arms. "If you consider me a partner, welcome him as you would welcome me." Not much wiggle room in that. I imagine Philemon himself reading the letter aloud to the church family, then lifting his eyes to see them all staring at him. What would he do?

I imagine Philemon himself reading the letter aloud to the church family, then lifting his eyes to see them all staring at him.

When Onesimus Comes to Our Church

We all like to think of our churches as friendly, starting with the hand-shakers at the front doors. Then the Lord sends us someone to stretch us. We gather as we do every Sunday—the elder brothers and sisters who have been doggedly diligent in the Father's fields for years, doing our family duties. Then we catch the faint strains of music and hear that there is a party at the Father's house for a wayward son or daughter come home. It sounds wonderful, and we are genuinely glad to join the party, but when the party is over, we need to learn to live with this new sibling.

I've been around long enough to see, more than once, an Onesimus come to church. Take Rich (name changed, but he has allowed me to tell his story). He'd been a beloved pastor elsewhere for sixteen years, but he consistently mishandled some relationships. He had become overbearing and manipulative. He said, "I had brokenness in my past that had greater impact than I understood. I had sin that was unresolved and undealt with . . . I was deceived, deceiving myself, and deceiving others. Things were not right in my heart and no matter how much I repented, or sought to change things, or discussed matters with accountability partners, things were not changing. I was unable to change."

Church leaders came to him, and he agreed to resign. It was devastating to him and his family. Rich and his wife had been converted in that church, and it was the only church family they'd ever known. Now they couldn't go back. He and his family came to our church family to recover. We agreed to care for them. Along with their previous congregation, we funded about two years of counseling for both Rich and his wife. They'd both been raised in terribly unhealthy homes and there was a lot of healing and rebuilding to do.

It was easy to love this family and, after a quiet year and a half, our elders felt we needed to find some way for Rich to serve the body. He and I had visited several times. He helped me think through a sermon series. We enjoyed "talking shop." I was touched by the hard work he was doing in his own life and the lessons he was learning about God's grace. But still, there *was* that past.

I was preaching a series of sermons, each drawn from a different text, focused on learning to understand and practice grace in the family of God. We decided it was a perfect time to invite Rich to preach. It was a deeply moving service. He focused on the way the early church welcomed the apostle Paul, and he shared some of his own story. Near the end of his sermon, Rich said, "It has been excruciating to recognize the pain I caused many others who I hurt over the years. I have lain in bed, or driven along the road, and had tears run down my face as I remembered this pain and wondered what God would have for me. And in all of this I thought of Paul and who he was and who he became. How did he get there? How did he forgive himself and accept God's grace so that he could do the good works God had for him? How could this great persecutor of the church become its most effective spokesperson?"

He concluded with words Onesimus might have used: "For all of us this morning [who are] wrestling with what God has for us, the message of grace cries out to us, 'You are not good enough for the cross, but the cross was good enough for you.'" When Rich finished that morning there was a holy hush. Our church grew a little stronger for having Onesimus—I mean Rich—with us.

Brother Saul

Onesimus's situation struck close to home for Paul, a.k.a. Saul. Years before, when he had been knocked from his high horse and blinded by light on the road to Damascus, God sent Ananias to meet him. Acts 9:17 says, "Then Ananias went to the house and entered it. Placing his hands on Saul, he said, 'Brother Saul, the Lord—Jesus, who appeared to you on the road as you were coming here—has sent me so that you may see again and be filled with the Holy Spirit.'" Did you catch that greeting? "*Brother* Saul." I wonder if that struck almost as hard as the light.

Saul spent several days with the disciples in Damascus, who must have been at least a little jittery to have a man with such a violent reputation in their fellowship. "When he came to Jerusalem, he tried to join the disciples, but they were all afraid of him, not believing that he really was a disciple. But Barnabas took him and brought him to the apostles. He told them how Saul on his journey had seen the Lord and that the Lord had spoken to him, and how in Damascus he had preached fearlessly in the name of Jesus" (Acts 19:26–27). Barnabas, the Son of Encouragement, was the church's best agent of grace. Barnabas was to Paul what Paul asked Philemon to be for Onesimus. Pass it on.

There is always a risk when we open our doors to the likes of Saul or Onesimus. The stories don't always turn out so well. Grace, by its very nature, doesn't come with guarantees. At the very end of Philemon's letter Paul sends greetings from his companions in Rome. Among them is Demas. But some time later, in his last letter, 2 Timothy, Paul writes, "Demas, because he loved this world, has deserted me and has gone to Thessalonica" (4:10). A heartbreaker, to be sure. Still, while we must be vigilant, the church should gamble on grace.

> **While we must be vigilant, the church should gamble on grace.**

Fresh Starts Refresh Hearts

Early in his letter, Paul remembered how Philemon had "refreshed the hearts of the Lord's people." Then, after his appeal, he says, "refresh my heart in Christ." When a church welcomes an Onesimus or a prodigal we are all refreshed. Imagine the holy moment when Philemon, greathearted as he was, embraced Onesimus while the church watched. I'm confident that Philemon did forgive Onesimus because God was at work in this story, "being confident of this, that he who began a good work in you will carry it on to completion until the day of Christ Jesus" (Phil. 1:6).

Imagine the relief and rest that would have come to the Philippian church if Euodia and Syntache did come to "the same mind in the Lord." As Peter said, "Love covers over a multitude of sins." I have watched sharp and painful conflicts dissolved by grace. There is a kind of collective sigh of relief and gratitude among all who know what's been going on.

Gordon MacDonald said, "The world can do almost anything as well as or better than the church. You need not be a Christian to build houses, feed the hungry, or heal the sick. There is only one thing the world cannot do. It cannot offer grace."[1] We first learn to show grace at home, in our congregations.

This story of Philemon, Onesimus, Paul and the Colossian church is a pretty typical church family story. It is a story saturated with God-given love and loyalty, just like Ruth. God arranges divine coincidences to position the household of God for grace, just as with Ruth's story. The benediction of Paul's letter to Philemon is fulfilled: "The grace of the Lord Jesus Christ be with your spirit" (v. 25). Fresh starts refresh hearts.

The Home of Discipleship

The work of the church is to be and to make disciples of Jesus Christ. What happened in Philemon's house church when Onesimus returned was discipleship. God had undoubtedly prepared them all for that moment, with Paul's letter being the final lesson before the test. They were learning what it means to follow Christ. Joseph Hellerman writes, "Spiritual formation occurs primarily in the context of community. . . . Long-term interpersonal relationships are the crucible of genuine progress in the Christian life. People who stay also grow. People who leave do not grow."[2]

Discipleship is not a solitary endeavor. There are certainly private struggles and personal lessons, but ultimately Jesus makes disciples in the environment of the church-home. Ephesians 4 spells out the typical pattern. From the parade of heaven-bound captives of grace, Jesus plucks out some to give as gifts to the church. Verses 11–13 say, "So Christ himself gave the apostles, the prophets, the evangelists, the pastors and teachers, to equip his people for works of service, so that the body of Christ may be built up until we all reach unity in the faith and in the knowledge of the Son of God and become mature, attaining to the whole measure of the fullness of Christ."

I call those four kinds of gift-people "Wordworkers," because each delivers God's Word in a particular kind of way. Through them the Word is embedded by the Holy Spirit in believers' minds and hearts. In turn, the believers are expected to serve their brothers and sisters in the church and beyond. One inevitable effect of this service is that the believers are stretched and tested—and sometimes fail. This, in turn, drives us back again to God's Word to grow in grace and truth, all within the bonds of our Christian family. The gradual outcome, as Paul says, is "that *the body of Christ* may be built up until *we all reach unity* in the faith and in the knowledge of the Son of God and become mature. . . ." Discipleship is not intended to be a solitary endeavor. It can only happen in the body of Christ, only in the unity of our church-home.

Picture that process in Philemon's life and church, as well as in Onesimus's. They surely had been taught about Christian love and grace. They had come to think of one another as brothers and sisters. Then Philemon reads aloud Paul's letter to him, as well as his letter to the Colossian church. I imagine him finishing, looking up and seeing every eye in the place on him, as if to say, "Well, *now* what are you going to do?" That is a discipleship moment. And such things happen constantly in the life of God's household. A decision must be made but not everyone is on the same page. Now what are you going to do? A new and difficult person starts attending. Now what are you going to do? A brother is unemployed. Now what are you going to do? Those decisions are the cutting edge of discipleship.

I think of Sue (name changed). Twenty years ago she returned from a stint as a missionary in Eastern Europe. Team struggles there exacerbated her depression. When she returned to the States she took a break from everything missions- and church-related. "I was broken," she said. "Being an out-of-church Christian caused me to have a different view of 'church.' The rose-colored glasses I previously wore were irreparably broken. I saw that church is painful for many. After a decade and a half of sincerely trying, I gave up. I quit looking. Except I couldn't. I needed to find fellowship."

She began to pray, "Lord, please lead me to the church You would like me to attend." She tried a friend's church. She said, "The first time I walked into Imago Dei I felt at home. I felt my heart leap for joy. The Spirit of the Lord was upon this place. I found what I was looking for all along: a church that was outward looking, caring not only for its members but also the community right there and the world at large. I felt welcomed from the start. I felt that this was a place where I could fit in and grow and be a part of something bigger than myself. Discipleship is built into everything this church does. In fact, the first class I took was a discipleship class for Christians who had been out of church for a while! So helpful, and it has allowed me to help others suffering my former plight."

The Rest of the Story

Around AD 100 the bishop of Antioch (where Jesus' disciples were first called Christians) was a man named Ignatius. He was imprisoned for his faith in Christ and sent to Rome to face the wild beasts in the Coliseum. He was eventually martyred there around AD 107.

At one stop on his journey to Rome, the church in Ephesus sent a delegation with their bishop to encourage Ignatius. Soon after, Ignatius wrote them a letter, which still survives. He thanked them for sending their bishop "whose love surpasses words. . . . I pray that you may love him with a love according to Jesus Christ, and that you may all be like him."[3]

That bishop's name was Onesimus. It's possible it wasn't the same Onesimus, but the timing fits. The bishop of Ephesus prior to Onesimus was Timothy, another spiritual son of Paul. Ephesus and Colossae were near each other. Not only that, many scholars believe that the first time the letters of Paul were collected was around AD 100 in Ephesus, where Bishop Onesimus led the church. Which could explain how this little gem of a letter that changed the life of a slave named

Onesimus found its way into the Scriptures (in God's providence of course)!

To consider:

Who has God brought to your church who required a stretch of grace?

In your own experience, how has persevering in a church when it might have been easier to leave affected your Christian maturity?

PART TWO

Interior Design:

The Spiritual Art of Decorating a Church Home

Jeanette Mix wanted to create a unique, upscale hotel in Stockholm, Sweden. She worked with Ilse Crawford, a "rock star" interior decorator. They looked at many buildings throughout Scandinavia and settled on a large home built in 1913, a time in Scandinavia when, according to Crawford, "the home became the focus for arts and life. The everyday was something that was celebrated and delightful. So one of the core principles was moving away from opulent luxury to a notion that luxury is attention. It's care."

Did you get that? "Luxury is attention. It's care."

I learned about this extraordinary project in a Netflix

Original documentary about Crawford.[1] Seeing the pictures of her finished work, you'd never guess you were looking at a hotel. Comfortable furniture, bookshelves, interesting touchable decorations, warm lighting. The kitchen is open to view, just as it is in our homes, with a long wooden table that invites guests to sit down for a snack or a chat. Crawford explains, "We wanted. . . . to make a place where, the minute you walked in, you just felt relaxed and as though you belonged. A home. Ett Hem: *a home*. When we came up with the name—*Ett Hem*—it all fell into place."

Are you beginning to see why this caught my attention? I started seeing the hotel *Ett Hem* as a metaphor for our congregation. We'd worked to communicate *home* through the ways we decorated our church, especially our foyer space. But Ilse Crawford's ideas had me thinking about how our church family presents our self. What is our congregation's *interior* design?

My wife and I visited an exciting church recently. It was a large and thriving campus. The music had already started when we arrived. The worship center was very dark, so an usher used her flashlight to show us to our seats. We could barely see other people. The stage was professionally lit, the music was performed well, and the words were excellent. Yet as I listened, I could not hear many others singing. I realized, of course, that this church was working from a very different model than the church as home. Their interior design (I mean their spirit, not their building or furnishings) communicated something entirely different. Frankly, the darkness and the volume of the music diluted a sense of personal connections. It was isolating.

Ilse Crawford explained that in the design of *Ett Hem*, "every decision came back to how does it feel, how is it run in a normal home. So we got rid of that formality, those boundaries [typical in a luxury hotel]. Not only do they take up space, they also make people behave differently. . . . [We chose] *to focus on the moment, on making the ordinary extraordinary, making the normal special. What happens when we do that is that it makes us much more open to each other and much closer"* (italics added).

In the following chapters, I hope to show you how a church family approaches our spiritual interior decorating—the approaches to ministry and life together that make the ordinary extraordinary and the normal special, the things that make us *ett hem*, a home.

6

God's Family at Rest

Paul Tournier, the pioneering Christian psychologist, wrote of a young man who came to see him. They sat by Tournier's fireside, his customary place of counseling, and the young man told him "of the anxiety that never left him, and which at times turned to panic and to flight." At one point the young man looked up at Tournier and said, "Basically, I'm always looking for a place—for somewhere to be."[1]

Ernest Hemingway wrote a short story set in Spain entitled "The Capital of the World." That short story begins by telling "about a father who came to Madrid and inserted an advertisement in the personal columns of *El Liberal* which said: PACO MEET ME AT HOTEL MONTANA NOON TUESDAY ALL IS FORGIVEN PAPA and how a squadron of Guardia Civil had to be called out to disperse the eight hundred young men who answered the advertisement."

Jesus' story of the prodigal son and waiting father is to me the most precious story He ever told. One Sunday morning, the lady at the Mobil station where I stopped for coffee asked what I was going to talk about that day. "I'm talking about the story of the prodigal son," I said. "You know that story, don't you?" She had never heard of it. I told her the story almost verbatim. When I came to that tenderest of verses, "But while he was still a long way off, his father saw him and was filled with compassion for him; he ran to his son, threw his arms around him and kissed him" (Luke 15:20), tears came to her eyes. "That's how God feels about you," I said.

A lot of people are "always looking for a place—for somewhere to be."

A Place of Rest

We often think of home as where you go to relax after a long day; the place to kick your shoes off, put on something comfortable, grab a snack and settle back in your chair. Our church home isn't really like that. It *is* a place of rest, but not that kind of rest exactly. Naomi, having just returned to Bethlehem, told Ruth, "I must find a home for you" (Ruth 3:1). The Hebrew means, "a place of rest," of security and love.

For fifteen hundred years of seventh days God embedded the idea of Sabbath rest in His people in preparation for Jesus Christ. Then Jesus issued this sweet invitation in Matthew 11:28–30, "Come to me, all you who are weary and burdened, and I will give you rest. Take my yoke upon you and learn from me, for I am gentle and humble in heart, and you will find rest for your souls. For my yoke is easy and my burden is light." God's Sabbath could now be embedded in our hearts. We could know the Lord of the Sabbath.

That isn't only a *personal* promise. It means that *together* we are Sabbath people, not because we take it easy one day a week but because we have all been given peace in our hearts through Christ. Whatever *our* lot, thou hast taught *us* to say, "It is well, it is well with *our* souls." We are a family living where rest reigns.

There are congregations that are *rest-averse*. The worst are those where legalism demands sacrifices to prove devotion, even though God has said, "*I desire mercy, not sacrifice.*"[2] The church may preach the gospel but their people are conditioned to believe that their Father is seldom happy with them unless they try harder. They assume He always wants more and better.

Other church families are trained to value activity or enthusiasm as the measure

When busyness and stirred-up excitement aren't rooted in souls at rest, they simply wear God's people out.

of spiritual vitality. Go, go, rah, rah. But when busyness and stirred-up excitement aren't rooted in souls at rest, they simply wear God's people out. As they say, "There's no rest for the weary." Peter Walsh, a guru of uncluttered houses, wrote, "Your home should be the antidote to stress, not the cause of it."[3] Church leaders should remember that. A church family that is well rested displays their "restedness" in various ways. Here are three.

Worship Displays Our Rest

Psalm 92 is the only psalm identified as "A psalm. A song. For the Sabbath day." Here's a lyric for God's well-rested people. It begins,

It is good to praise the LORD
    and make music to your name, O Most High,

. . . .

to the music of the ten-stringed lyre
    and the melody of the harp.

For you make me glad by your deeds, LORD;
    I sing for joy at what your hands have done.

Our God-satisfied souls make beautiful music together. Paul says, "Be filled with the Spirit, speaking to one another with psalms, hymns, and songs from the Spirit. Sing and make music from your heart to the Lord, always giving thanks to God the Father for everything, in the name of our Lord Jesus Christ" (Eph. 5:18–20). In worship, rested souls strengthen one another by delighting in God together. The worship of the well rested, spiritually speaking, calms and quiets those who are agitated and weary.

When our worship setting isolates people in theater darkness or surrounds them with music so loud they can't hear their own voices, they lose the sense of being a family at worship. The contemporary hymn writer Keith Getty, in an interview with Ed Stetzer, said, "What could be more inviting than the joy of a community singing with joy and love to one another? What could be more radical than song breaking down generational, socioeconomic, and political ideology barriers for the sheer delight of singing to one another about how much greater Christ is? And in a society so contrived, what is more authentic than people pouring all their passion into singing to the Lord because of what Christ has done through the Cross and Resurrection? That's a unity worth striving for."[4]

Psalm 92's Sabbath song concludes in verses 12–15,

The righteous will flourish like a palm tree,
    they will grow like a cedar of Lebanon;
planted in the house of the LORD,
    they will flourish in the courts of our God.
They will still bear fruit in old age,
    they will stay fresh and green,
proclaiming, "The LORD is upright;
    he is my Rock, and there is no wickedness in him."

God's presence is like a greenhouse for the righteous, even the elderly righteous. The fruit we bear breaks out in song. The worship of Sabbath people is like Miracle-Gro for our hearts.

I love this psalm's mention of older believers. I feel sorry for churches that don't have them. What a mistake for a church to think that our older people should be seen and not heard. (Judging from some church websites, they aren't even seen.) Our congregation has many who are over sixty. They are *not* rigid or judgmental, contrary to the bad rap older people get sometimes. They have stayed "fresh and green." When Joyce, who is in her eighties, reads Scripture, she brings a deliberate thoughtfulness that no one younger could convey. Recently a student told me, "When I think of grace, I don't think of my pastor or youth pastor. I think of the old ladies in my church."

Saints young and old enrich worship with testimonies

of God's love and power in our lives. Like a family gathered around the dinner table, we share with one another in worship about our experiences with the Lord. Often our songs are testimonies gathered into one voice. Other times we are all ears as a brother or sister tells us their story of God's goodness. In our congregation, we occasionally use finish-the-sentence testimonies. We give a starter, like *"One difference the Lord has made in my life is . . ."* and then people stand and speak, popcorn-like. Family worship includes family stories of our Father's care and our Elder Brother's salvation.

The table, of course, is another focal point of Sabbath people. It is a multipurpose meal of thanksgiving, of communion with the Lord and one another, of remembering Jesus' sacrifice for us, and of hope for our homecoming. As a rule, Christians observe the Lord's Supper with other believers, not alone. Together, we time travel back to the Passover and to the dark night of Jesus' last supper. But we also receive the elements as hors d'oeuvres for our wedding banquet when we will join Jesus and all our brothers and sisters in the Great Feast long promised by God. There, together at the table, we are nourished and refocused. In some mystical way we are joined by Jesus. Communion is the very gathering place of our fellowship with the Lord.

Confession and assurance of God's forgiveness are often left out of worship services, but these, too, are precious expressions of souls at rest. Recently I was a visitor in a service where a thoughtful prayer of confession was offered. As I listened I found myself offloading not only my lurking sins but also simply reorienting to God's mercy in my time of need. That prayer did what singing couldn't do.

A benediction is the very pronouncement of rest, God's blessing upon His people. I'm baffled as to why pastors exchange this sweet priestly privilege to say, as if we were leaving a coffee shop, "See you next week." To bestow the Aaronic blessing in Numbers 6:24–26, for example, ("The LORD bless you and keep you . . .") is to proclaim to God's people their birthright in Christ. It is like parents who send their kids out the door by looking them right in the eyes and saying, "Remember who you are."

Corporate Prayer Displays Our Rest

If our souls rest as Jesus reveals the Father to us, then praying together is an eye-opening experience (even when our eyes are closed). Moses said in Deuteronomy 4:7, "What other nation is so great as to have their gods near them the way *the LORD our God is near us* (italics added) whenever we pray to him?" Jesus taught us to begin praying, "Our Father in heaven . . ." (Matt. 6:9) because we are His beloved children.

Paul echoed Moses in Philippians 4:5–7. "*The Lord is near,*" he wrote. "Do not be anxious about anything, but in every situation, by prayer and petition, with thanksgiving, present your requests to God. And the *peace of God*, which transcends all understanding, will guard your hearts and your minds in Christ Jesus." Or as Jesus put it, "Come to me, all you who are weary and burdened, and I will give you rest." In prayer, we position ourselves for peace, casting on Jesus our wearisome concerns. These are not only

In prayer we position ourselves for peace, casting on Jesus our wearisome concerns.

private promises. They are for us as a church family, gathered together in prayer.

In my experience, it isn't difficult to convince Christians that we should pray, but to persuade them that we should pray *together* is another story. Sometimes, as when we send out an urgent concern to our church via email, we pray together even though we're in many different places. But the family of God needs to gather in the same place for prayer, too. Jesus wasn't only speaking of church discipline issues when He said in Matthew 18:19–20, "Truly I tell you that if two of you on earth agree about anything they ask for, it will be done for them by my Father in heaven. For where two or three gather in my name, there am I with them." That, too, is family talk.

Acts 4 tells of the arrest of Peter and John and their eventual release. When they returned "to their own people. . . . they raised their voices *together* in prayer to God" (vv. 4:23–24). After a Scripture-fortified prayer for boldness, "the place where they were meeting was shaken. And they were all filled with the Holy Spirit and spoke the word of God boldly" (v. 31). I've never been in a prayer meeting where the room shook, but I have certainly sensed God's presence and answers many times as we've buckled down and prayed earnestly together.

Many of the people in our congregation pray together in their small groups, but those prayers are usually for one another. A few years ago, I felt our people needed to make a higher priority of praying together for the larger concerns of our church, and especially for more effective outreach. We had a monthly Sunday evening prayer service but attendance was limited. So we started *First, Prayer* on the first Sunday morning of each month instead of our usual adult education classes. We began the times with a short account of one of the great revivals, detailing how it was preceded by prayer. That built up our faith. Simply by changing the time and making our unified prayer a priority, our attendance more than doubled.

Our prayers together (as well as personally) should boldly lay hold of God's help, His restoring grace, His wisdom, and His power to push open doors of unbelief. To bear one another's burdens we must pray. To worship is to pray. To weep before God is to pray. To puzzle out God's Word is to pray.

A few years ago I heard an idea about praying for healing during the worship service, which we use now every few weeks. We invite everyone to stand—except those who would like prayer for healing of body, mind or spirit. We ask those who are near someone seated to lay hands on them. No one explains his or her particular need; they just sit. Then an elder prays for everyone collectively. We take special care in thinking through this prayer, to undergird it with Scripture and to come to it confident in God's grace and power. Before we tried this, I was afraid it would be off-putting to visitors, but I now think it is an especially potent thing for them to observe. After all, what better way for them to sense that "God is really among you"? (1 Cor. 14:25).

One Saturday night many years ago I was called to the hospital. One of our teens had attempted suicide by swallowing a bottle of pills. She was unconscious. Her doctor that night was a godly man who prayed with the family. She would live, he said, but there was no telling what kind of damage may have been done. The next morning, I certainly planned to pray for our girl in my pastoral prayer but before the first service I decided on a different approach. I explained the situation to the church family and asked people to cluster and pray for her. The murmur of those urgent prayers was beautiful. An hour later, as I walked out of the auditorium at the end of the service I was met by a brother who'd just taken a call from the girl's nurse, who happened to be from our church. Our church's daughter had awakened while we were praying and was in perfect health.

Resting at Jesus' Feet

The story of Martha and Mary in Luke 10:38–42 is the story of two sisters, each distracted by Jesus. Most of us have a picture of Martha—one of those kitchen commandos, the queen of the table. "Make yourselves comfortable," she says. "I'll get dinner going." But even for Martha, Jesus' visit was asking a lot. Thirteen men for dinner. No fridge, no microwave.

Mary turned out to be a sharp disappointment to Martha because instead of helping (as the Proverbs 31 woman surely would have), she just sat at Jesus' feet and listened. In a controlled burn, Martha said, "Lord, don't you care that my sister has left me to do the work by myself? Tell her to help me!"

Verse 40 says Martha "was distracted by all the preparations that had to be made [*diakonia*]," and then she complained, "My sister has left me to do all the work [*diakoneo*] by myself." Sometimes the epistles translate that word *ministry.* That's what being responsible gets you sometimes. Serving Jesus and His disciples can get very stressful—ask any pastor. We'd love to just sit and listen to the Lord (in theory, anyway), but we have work to do. Not just busywork either. Real responsibilities. Duties. Work that God Himself assigned to us. We're not just making widgets here! After all, we're serving Jesus!

> "Martha, Martha," the Lord answered, "you are worried and upset about many things, but few things are needed—or indeed only one. Mary has chosen what is better, and it will not be taken away from her."

I'd always pictured Mary as a dreamy-eyed young woman with her head in the clouds. The kind who today would hide and read a Jane Austen book when the table needed to be set; whose sister would call her three times, and then she'd look up and say, *"Whaaat?"* Contemplative, inward, impractical. But there's no good reason to see her that way. Mary knew all about the demands of hospitality and took them as seriously as every other woman in their community. But where Martha was distracted by *serving* Jesus, Mary was distracted by *listening* to Him. While Martha was *attending* to Jesus, Mary gave Him her *attention*.

A well-rested church family learns to sometimes step back from serving Jesus so that Jesus can serve us. It's interesting that Luke doesn't tell us what Jesus was saying that held Mary's rapt attention. I'm sure of this, though: He was bringing rest to her soul as He did for the others who listened. His words lifted up heavy yokes of duty and gently unloaded the burdens of each soul.

Imagine preparing to read Scripture on a Sunday morning by asking the Holy Spirit to invest that reading with the same gentle authority that captivated Mary. What if we asked Jesus to serve His people in the reading of the Bible to them? Who would you ask to read? How would you ask someone to prepare? I've heard Scripture read with such reverence and thoughtfulness that a hush settled over the room when it was over, as if Jesus Himself had been speaking.

As a preacher, I see my responsibility reflected in what Jesus did that day. Some sermons, of course, must make people squirm. Others are bugle calls to obedience and service. But most of the time I want my preaching to pull people from their distractions, from their burdens and weariness, even from their service, that they might be fed by Jesus and find, once again, rest for their souls. Romans teaches us that *law reveals but grace heals.* The problem is that it seems easier to preach moralism than mercy. It can be easier to hammer people from the pulpit than to heal them. No one who preaches Scripture well will produce irresponsible believers, but to preach God-given breathing space, God-given rest at Jesus' feet, is what gospel preaching does best.

Grace Dispenser

At its heart, serving Jesus is dispensing grace. That's what we want our church family to do. Go out and dispense grace in word and deed. But we cannot dispense grace if we do not let Jesus grace us. And for that we must be quiet and receptive.

Later I'll tell you about the Lenten season when I set out to practice listening prayer with every household in my congregation. During that time, I remember sitting in Nels and Karen's family room. They had a fire in the fireplace, soft music in the background. They are wonderful Christians who had a tough year. Out of the quiet the Lord brought to my mind uniquely personal words of direction and affirmation for each of them. I'd speak and then we'd be still for a while. Then another

"We spend so much time serving . . . going . . . doing. And here Jesus just came to be with us."

prayer. After about a half hour, I looked up and held my hands out over them as I did at the end of everyone's session, and pronounced the Aaronic blessing. "The LORD bless you and keep you," I began. They looked up, tears streaming down their faces. "The LORD make his face shine upon you and be gracious to you." They drank in God's blessing, their birthright. "The LORD turn his face toward you and give you peace" (Num. 6:24–26). They just sat there, breathing deeply, wiping the tears. Then Nels whispered, "We spend so much time serving . . . going . . . doing." He shook his head. "And here Jesus just came to be with us."

To consider:

Would you describe your church as a place of rest for souls?

I identify three spheres of spiritual rest—worship, corporate prayer, and sitting at Jesus' feet to receive His grace and truth. Which are your church's strengths? Weaknesses?

7

Company's Coming

Growing up, the news "company's coming" was a signal to prepare. We had to clean our rooms. Mom made a cake or cookies. We had a sense of anticipation. Church friends or neighbors were going to join us, or perhaps relatives from far away. They were special. We wanted them to feel at home. So it is with our church family. Let's be ready. Company's coming!

When visitors come to our church it is dangerously tempting to think of them as means to an end—the goal being the growth of our church. I recall a visiting Navy seaman from Great Lakes Naval Base near us, telling me how he'd gone to other churches but when they found out he would only be around a few months they didn't pay much attention to him. Don't welcome guests into our church family so that our church can grow. Welcome them because we want to love them.

"God Is Really Among You!"

Part of the seeker-sensitive movement in churches was to make "unchurched Harry and Mary" comfortable if they came through the door. Songs were easy to pick up. There were great visuals and intriguing dramatic sketches. Instead of sermons, there were talks. Everything that happened on the stage was dynamic and well rehearsed. Visitors could be mostly observers so that they weren't scared away from church before they even heard the good news. Everything was done to put people at ease and to hold their attention. Whether or not we adopt this philosophy of ministry, many congregations have benefited from this sensitivity to unchurched people among us. In the past we were often oblivious to how foreign a church service was to people. We made it hard to come in.

That said, we may have missed what is most important. When Paul first wrote to the church in the pagan city of Corinth, he gave them instructions about their worship services. Some people who spoke in tongues had become arrogant about their gift. But Paul tells the church that the gift that was most valuable was prophesying, i.e., declaring God's word and will. He writes in 1 Corinthians 14:24–25,

> But if an unbeliever or an inquirer comes in while everyone is prophesying, they are convicted of sin and are brought under judgment by all, as the secrets of their hearts are laid bare. So they will fall down and worship God, exclaiming, "God is really among you!"

The scene here is of an unsaved visitor coming into the typical worship service. The prophecies expressed by members of the church family were likely a combination of both Spirit-directed encouragement and warnings against sin. I suspect they were anchored in Old Testament passages. They may have been very specific, even personal. But rather than mere moral scolding, these prophecies had a powerful immediacy about them, striking unchurched Harry and Mary as personal words from God, laying bare the secrets of their hearts! They fell to their knees in worship, vividly aware that "God is really among you!" Worship services were not showrooms for church shoppers. They were appointments with the living God!

Paul continues in verse 26, "When you come together, each of you has a hymn, or a word of instruction, a revelation, a tongue or an interpretation. Everything must be done so that the church may be built up." Do you see why Christians gather? "*So that the church may be built up,*" and while that is happening the unbelievers and inquirers witness God's life and love among us. Where else will they see God's family life if not among us?

Consider a different picture. The Bible describes believers together as the living temple of God. Ephesians 2:22 says, "In him [Christ] you too are being built together to become a dwelling in which God lives by his Spirit." First Corinthians 3:16 echoes, "Don't you know that you yourselves are God's temple and that God's Spirit dwells in your midst?"

When we travel, I like to visit historic church buildings. The 350-year-old Bruton Parish Church in Williamsburg, Virginia. Rockefeller Chapel at the University of Chicago. St. Patrick's Cathedral in New York. Mission San Juan Capistrano in Southern California. The tiny log Chapel of the Transfiguration at the base of the Teton Mountains in Wyoming. There is always a sacred hush in these places. But imagine *we're* the temple which spiritual tourists visit on Sunday. Whatever it is that they think they are looking for, we must be sure they encounter the Lord among us.

It is easy to forget that even our worship is *God's* gift to *us* before it becomes our gift to Him. Were it not for the working of the Holy Spirit, our songs and sermons would not get off the ground. We and our guests would go home unchanged. Therefore, our preparation for worship is crucial. I don't mean our rehearsals or sermon study. I mean how we beseech our triune God to display His grace and truth when we gather.

God is certainly not reluctant to be among His people nor is He reclusive. But think how often God's people in the Bible, oblivious to their terrible sins, presumed upon God's presence when, in fact, He refused to be among them. Their worship was a fiction, all form and no function. The Lord God makes His presence felt among His people when we humble ourselves before Him and pray, not only *during* our worship services but *before*. We must pray in advance of our services to tune our hearts to sing God's grace. Sometimes, I'm sure, Jesus stands at our door knocking, only to be ignored, not because we don't want Him, but because we are too preoccupied with our worship stuff to welcome Him in. Through our preparatory prayers, the Holy Spirit attunes people to the presence of God.

"How They Love One Another"

The second priority is that our guests must sense that God's people love one another and them. After all, our love is how people know we're Christians. This can be tricky. One woman told me that the first time they came to our church she felt like she walked into someone else's family reunion. That's *almost* good. She saw our love for one another but wasn't sure how to break in to the family. When we love being with our brothers and sisters it is difficult to even *see* the guests among us unless we make it our priority.

We all know how oblivious our people can be to our guests. After a service recently I saw a first-time visitor across the foyer standing alone. *Somebody talk to him!* I thought. I started dodging and weaving through the crowd to get to him. When I did, we chatted a moment and I introduced him to Dave, who was standing nearby. But we almost ignored the guy!

For our guests to have those two powerful impressions— God's presence and our love—we must pray because these are the Holy Spirit's business. Perhaps we need to take specific steps, like recruiting prayer volunteers to form a worship preparation team. I call ours the Prelude Prayer Group. Ask them to pray several times each week for these two specific needs: (1) that all who come to the service(s) would sense that "God is really among you," and (2) that it would be evident that these believers love one another and we love our guests. If possible, establish a time on Sunday morning when at least some of these people can meet to pray with one another before everything starts.

God *wants* to make His presence known among us! He *wants* people to realize how unique our love is for one another! God is hospitable. We are His family. Hospitality belongs in church. Company's coming!

Web Masters

Once I watched one of our elders leading a group of a dozen newcomers to the church. They sat in a circle. He gave the first person a big ball of red yarn and invited him to begin to tell his story—where he grew up, what his family was like, and so on. When someone else in the circle shared a similar experience they'd break in. "My dad was a postal carrier, too," they might say. The first person would stop, hold on to the end of the yarn, and pass the ball across the circle to that person. It continued like that as people discovered things they had in common, and after a while there was this red-yarn web linking the people in the circle. The ice had been broken.

Churches do all manner of things to make visitors feel welcome—preferred parking, greeters, gifts, Welcome Centers, gathering places with great coffee, and on and on. Those things are all well and good—but how do we love them and bring them into the circles of our church family life?

When I talk with people who have visited a number of churches the number one thing I hear from them is, *no one talked to me.* The same in big churches and little churches. There may have been greeters but no one else seemed to notice a visitor. One woman, whose husband has preached in dozens of churches, told of a large church where her husband was preaching. She said, "I stood in the middle of the foyer with people rushing by and bumping into me. No one said a word, not even 'excuse me.'"

People can find a church where they like the music, preaching, and kids' programs. They can settle in and attend regularly, but *until they are known* they aren't part of the church envisioned by Scripture. Until they are connected to others as brothers and sisters in Christ, they will be like distant cousins. Pastors and church leaders must help weave them into the church's web of relationships.

We might start with a newcomers' lunch or an Explorers'
Class. I learned a long time ago that it is easiest for new
people to make friends with other new people, but that isn't
always possible. We like to invite several new people over to
our home, along with one or two of our church families to
try to create some relational Stickum. Pastors should monitor
how newer people are settling in. Have they joined a ministry
or a small group? Are their kids making friends? Do you see
them visiting with others on Sunday mornings?

Teach Your Church
Family to Watch for Guests

I pushed the wrong elevator button at a Marriott Hotel and
went to the basement where the staff kept their supplies and
equipment. When the elevator door opened, I saw a 3' x 4' sign
on the wall. Big letters said, "The 15/5 Rule." Then, "When
a guest comes within 15 feet, stop—make eye contact and
smile. Within 5 feet, we engage and verbally greet the guest."
A housekeeper looked at me curiously when I stopped to take
a picture. "That's a great rule," I said, "I'm going to show that
to my church." I have, and they immediately took to it. We
put just "15/5" among other notices on our foyer monitors to
remind people without tipping off our guests to our plan.

As I walk around before and after our service, I seek out
new folks, as many pastors do. When I meet someone, I chat a
few minutes and then I almost always say, "Let me introduce
you to _____," and I put someone nearby on the spot.
Knowing the people as I do, I choose people who will extend

a kind welcome. Then, as they are greeting one another, I walk away. People get the idea.

Greeters and Ushers

Don't undervalue the ministry of greeters and ushers who can connect quickly with those who come through our doors. They set the tone. We don't just want glad-handers. We want people who are kind. I often pray on Sundays that we will be more than friendly; that we will make friends. It starts with these people.

Doug heads up these teams in our church. One day he told me that he'd like to pray with his teams before they begin but that it was just too difficult to get them all together. I suggested that he write a short prayer and give it to his people as he connects with them on Sunday mornings. He does that, writing a new prayer from time to time. This is one of them:

> Father, we thank you for the opportunity to come together today as a team to serve our church. You are the Good Shepherd. You are kind. You welcome those who seek you and those who are lost and not sure what they seek.
>
> As folks arrive today, help us to greet everyone with the same kindness and the same open arms you extend to us. Give us the strength to put aside our own problems and focus our energy completely on all of those who enter our church home. Give us the patience to spend extra time with those who have questions or special needs, and bless us with the knowledge to guide them where they need to go.
>
> We pray in Jesus' name. Amen.

"Would You Guys Be Available to Come Over to Our house?"

When we were just beginning in the ministry an older pastor told us that we would be going to a lot of weddings. "Figure out a gift that you can give to every couple," he said, "and buy a supply." One of our most precious possessions was our Guest Book. In fact, over our forty-six years of marriage we've filled about six of them with thousands of names. So we give a guest book to newlyweds. I write in each one, reminding the couple that this book can be a ledger of God's blessings to them. "And who knows," I always write, "somewhere in these pages you might even collect an angel's autograph." At the bottom of the page I write, "Do not forget to entertain strangers, for by so doing some people have shown hospitality to angels without knowing it"(see Heb. 13:2). Author's paraphrase. Hospitality welcomes people, not only into our homes, but into our church family.

When my wife and I have new people to our home we almost always follow the same pattern. Once everyone has arrived we ask our guests to tell us a little about their background, how they found our church, and what one of their first impressions of our congregation was. Then we take a break for refreshments and stand back. We don't have to do much after that because people cluster in the living room and kitchen to visit. Pretty soon, friendships are forming. (Be sure they have nametags. You might send everyone an email afterward, again giving all the names.) I can almost assure you that the next Sunday these folks will be talking with one another.

Names Matter

Sometimes churches forget that names matter. I remember talking to a staff member of a church of about four hundred. Their staff had gone through the church directory and realized that half the people listed were unknown personally to any of them. That's not a healthy family.

At the end of Paul's letter to the Roman church he mentions thirty-three names, each precious to Paul.

> I commend to you our sister Phoebe, a deacon of the church in Cenchreae. . . . Greet Priscilla and Aquila, my co-workers in Christ Jesus. They risked their lives for me. Not only I but all the churches of the Gentiles are grateful to them. Greet also the church that meets at their house.
>
> Greet my dear friend Epenetus, who was the first convert to Christ in the province of Asia. Greet Mary, who worked very hard for you. Greet Andronicus and Junia, my fellow Jews who have been in prison with me. They are outstanding among the apostles, and they were in Christ before I was. (Romans 16:1, 3–7)

He goes on to his "dear friend" Ampliatus, his "co-worker" Urbanus, Apelles, "whose fidelity to Christ has stood the test," Rufus, "chosen in the Lord, and his mother, who has been a mother to me, too," and others. He never asks how big the congregation is now. He just asks about the people, and sends greetings to them from eight specific people who were with him.

I grew up in a small rural church in South Dakota where it wasn't a problem to remember names. We knew a lot more about one another than names! The church I now serve in the northern suburbs of Chicago is different. We might have two hundred people on a Sunday morning, but the names keep changing. In a recent five-year period, we said goodbye to 261 people and welcomed 261 people. That's a lot of goodbyes and hellos, and those are a lot of names to learn. But if we're going to be a family, learning names is a priority. When I called Pat by name on her second Sunday, her eyes got wide. "How did you remember my name?" she asked. I didn't tell her that I work at it.

Learning someone's name is an introductory act of Christian love. We can't dismiss this duty by saying, "I'm just not good with names." If that's the case, then you'll just have to work harder at them. The next time folks show up in church, I want to call them by name because I am a shepherd and they may become my sheep.

Names are sticky. Once you learn someone's name, you can start attaching details to it: a hometown or a profession, a personality type or a testimony of faith. But without a name, you can't do much more than be an acquaintance.

Jo and Arthur were part of our church for just two years while he was in seminary. They'd been part of large churches in Singapore and Australia. They had loved those churches and admired their pastors, albeit from afar. When they left Village Church, Jo wrote of me in her blog, "He is the first shepherd on earth who knows my name. I will never forget the first time Pastor Lee called my name in the foyer the second Sunday we met. I was moved beyond words. I am truly thankful for a shepherding pastor who knows me." Names matter.

In a classic sermon on Romans 16 entitled, "When the Roll Is Called Down Here," Fred Craddock concluded with these words to pastors:

Write these words: "I thank my God for all my remembrance of you." Now write a name. Write another name, and another name, and another. Keep the list, because to you, it's not a list. In fact, the next time you move, hold on to that list. Even if you have to leave your car, and your library, and your furniture, and your typewriter, and everything else, take that list with you. In fact, when your ministry has ended and you leave the earth, take it with you.[1]

"Dying to Love Them"

Our work is just beginning when someone new starts coming more regularly. At first our goal is to make them feel at home. Next, we want to make them part of the family.

A couple of years ago, Jim and Jenn were given the opportunity, with very little notice, to adopt two young siblings. They already have three children who at the time were in high school, middle school, and elementary school, respectively. When Jim gathered the kids to tell them about this possibility, Jenn filmed it: Jim sitting in his easy chair, the three kids facing him in curious anticipation. "We've been approached about the possibility of adopting two children," he said. Eyebrows go up! After he explained the details he asked the kids what they thought. They replied, "I think that would be cool. It's exciting. I like the idea. I'm a little nervous." Jim said, "Obviously, this will change a lot for our family. We run the risk of a lot of emotional pain, which is what we're sometimes called to as Christians."

Later Jenn told me how they learned that there were not just two more children to manage, but exponentially more relational dynamics. She said that they certainly gained wonderful blessings in this process but there were also losses because it was disruptive to bring two children under age two into the family. Suddenly, the baby of the family wasn't the baby anymore. The older kids had to shoulder a lot more responsibility than they had bargained for. It hasn't always been easy. Some of those same dynamics play out in church when new people come into our family.

Paul teaches us about adoption as a result of our salvation. In Romans 8:15 he says, "the Spirit you received brought about your adoption to sonship. And by him we cry, 'Abba, Father.'" Like the Briggs family in chapter 1, our church family are all adoptees. We all come as orphans and prodigals, with our wounds and baggage, often unprepared for the self-sacrifice and care expected in the family of God. The people who come through our church doors and step into our church family aren't always a natural fit at first.

Part of pastoring, as with parenting, is helping our people welcome others to our family. Have you seen those YouTube videos of a little kid who finds out she's going to have a little brother and breaks out crying? Same thing with enfolding new folks into our community. I've heard things like, *"Why don't they control their kids?" "All that guy wants to talk about is prophecy." "She's always talking about how their old church was better."* Some new people don't seem to want to talk to anyone. Some want too much attention. But that is part of being a family who welcomes other adoptees. I find myself soothing concerns, making introductions, building bridges, and explaining people's back stories, because newcomers will only become part of our church family if they are known and loved.

My pastor friend Josh told me, "When our friends were

getting ready to adopt their first child, I asked them why they were doing it. Her response was: 'It's not because we think our family is so awesome. It's because we're dying to love them.' So I've grappled with what a church would look like that saw every guest the way [our friends] saw their son . . . dying to love them. That's family being family AND welcoming outsiders at the same time."

To consider:

Do you think visitors who come to your church sense that "God is really among you"? How could you enhance that impression?

If loving one another starts with knowing names, how could you encourage that without embarrassing your guests?

8

Personal Attention

My wife, Susan, comes from a Christian family of nine kids. They had lots of family times together around a long table. (Her father considered installing a drain down the middle to catch all the spilled milk.) But one thing Susan rarely got was time alone with both of her parents at the same time. In fact, she remembers only one occasion, and she remembers every detail. Seeing that each person in our church family gets personal attention is part of a church being a home.

I've heard that Eugene Peterson once said that next to the Bible, the church directory is the most important book in the pastor's study. Near the beginning of Peterson's book, *Five Smooth Stones for Pastoral Work*, he writes, "It is the unique property of pastoral work to combine two aspects of ministry: one, to represent the eternal Word and will of God; and, two, to do it among the idiosyncrasies of the local and the personal (the actual place where the pastor lives; the named people with whom he or she lives). If either aspect is slighted, good pastoral work fails to take place."[1]

The Pastor's Inefficient Imperative

Big churches have some disadvantages. As Mother Goose said,

> There was an old woman who lived in a shoe.
> She had so many children, she didn't know what to do.

Pastors can face that problem, especially in larger congregations. The rest of Mother Goose's rhyme is,

> She gave them some broth without any bread;
> And whipped them all soundly and put them to bed.

I suppose pastors, under the pressure of too many people, might feel that way sometimes.

That said, in small and medium-sized congregations, personal attention starts with a pastor. One-on-one pastoral care is every pastor's inefficient imperative. It invariably seems we could get more done if we were left alone to study or plan, or if we could be with a group of our people all at once to teach or worship or just eat together.

There is this powerful instinct to always shepherd the flock in bunches.

There is this powerful instinct to always shepherd the flock in bunches, in herds, because it seems patently obvious we'd get more done. But efficiency is a poor pastoral master.

We would hardly know Jesus if it weren't for all His personal encounters in the Gospels. Peter at his nets, Matthew at his tax table, Mary at Jesus' feet, the desperate centurion, the raving demoniac, Nicodemus, the woman at the well, the thief on the cross. Jesus met people one-on-one.

I wonder whether, in some divine miracle, a whole church has a sense of being shepherded well when only one or two actually had the shepherd's attention. The ninety-nine in the fold are better off—healthier, more content—when the one lost sheep is carried home to the flock. Heaven is certainly the happier for it.

Years ago, "Marv" would just drop by my office. No appointment. Just stick his nose in my door and strike up a conversation. (Not all pastors have gatekeepers.) He was needy. He really was. And it helped him to talk. It frustrated me to pieces, and sometimes I told him I was busy. I never felt those visits were very useful because he never seemed to get better but I eventually decided that what Jesus had me doing was washing Marv's feet.

Pastoral work is humbling. It's humbling because we so frequently feel inadequate but also because it is often such *small* work. A pastoral friend writes a birthday card to every person in his church. Small work. Another quietly prays through the church directory. Small work. We call on people and no one ever hears about it. We sit and make small talk with someone while trying not to worry about our unfinished sermon. Small work. We pray for a tenth grader's audition or a forty-five-year-old's job interview. We take a newcomer to lunch, or help arrange some funds for a sister with a need. Small work.

I can think of few Christians who have more opportunities to get rich slowly than pastors. When we were trudging down hospital corridors or going back to the church for evening counseling, when we were squeezing in a visit to a shut-in or meeting with a seventeen-year-old just to talk about school, we were bringing food to hungry hearts. We were inviting in strangers. We were clothing people—maybe in garments of white. We went into prisons, some with unseen bars, and jingled the keys of grace. "The King will reply, 'Truly I tell you, whatever you did for one of the least of these brothers and sisters of mine, you did for me'" (Matt. 25:40). It was so ordinary, so small, but look where it got us: "in his glory, and all the angels with him" (v. 31). This is what pastors do if we want to minister like Jesus. It is inefficient, to be sure, but that's how it is.[2]

Still, like my wife's parents, there is a limit to how much personal attention we can give. If a church is to be home, the siblings need to help care for one another.

"Getting to Know You; Getting to Know All About You"

Remember the four siblings who found one another through DNA searches? They had been related all along, even when they didn't know it. But once they found each other, they needed and wanted time together to begin to weave their lives together as a family should. Most of a believer's personal spiritual connections won't be just with their pastor. In fact, if the pastor is the only person who connects with someone on a spiritual level, they're in jeopardy. We all need to be an integral part of a body.

Usually people ease into close relationships. Church leaders need to help that happen. North Point Community Church in Atlanta also emphasizes the importance of environment to church life. They identify their strategy: "to create environments where people are encouraged and equipped to pursue intimacy with God, community with insiders, and influence with outsiders."[4] The church uses the analogy of moving through three rooms of a home. The foyer represents the environment where guests are greeted and made to feel welcome. The living room is where people get comfortable with others who have things in common with them. Their literature says, "these gatherings offer genuine opportunity to begin friendships." The kitchen is the family center, where deep relationships are formed and "where people meet regularly for Bible study and prayer, and commit to accountability, friendship and support. They are the safe place to open your heart, share your life, and ask tough questions."[4]

No matter how you structure this process of moving someone from guest to beloved family member, we need to provide ways for people to form deep Christian bonds. As I've mentioned, I grew up in a country church with sixty or seventy people, mostly farmers. Everyone knew everyone else very well. At one point in my life, I pastored a fairly large church where it became impossible for people to know everyone. In fact, I think I was the only person who did. (Although I admit that there were some kids I just renamed Buddy.) I realized, with the help of a church consultant, that if our church was to have strong relationships, we had to establish lots of what I thought of as little country churches within our big church. So instead of continuing our elective adult classes, we moved to an Adult Bible Fellowship model, oriented to life stages, where there was not only a teaching element, but also social events and ministry projects. These groups significantly strengthened relationships, but because of their size they didn't give opportunity for much intimacy. For that, we needed to foster small groups more aggressively.

Christian intimacy develops in small groups and mentoring relationships. In our country church we all knew each other well, but I don't think most folks knew each other deeply. I don't recall people talking candidly about their spiritual struggles. I remember kneeling on the hard wooden floor at Wednesday night prayer meeting to pray for missionaries or Vacation Bible School, but I wonder if we ever prayed for someone's heartache, a wayward child, or peace in a strained relationship. That's what needs to develop in small groups.

Personal Attention: A Small Group's Hinge Moment

I'll have a pastor friend of mine tell you about a small group he once led:

> A new couple named Tad and Sherri joined the group. For many months Sherri was totally silent. She would not say anything unless absolutely necessary. Her husband was very quiet as well. As time went on it became more and more evident that the Lord was working in their lives and that they were responding through their own personal Scripture readings and support for one another.
>
> After many months, Sherri shared that she was quite ill but they had no insurance. As she shared she began to sob almost uncontrollably. The group gathered around her, laid hands on her and fervently prayed. Some of us offered to connect her with the local free clinic in the next town. Her husband Tad shared that he was looking for a job where he could have benefits so she could have insurance. (They were both self-employed.) The group began to pray he'd get a job with an employer who could offer good benefits.

One day I said, "As a way to get to know one another, I'd like us all to share our faith journey." It took us a few weeks to get through all the stories of the group. Out of fear, Tad and Sherri waited to be the final people to share. When Tad shared, he shared about being sexually abused throughout his childhood. He was extremely transparent and emotional as he told his story. As an adult, when he tried to confront his abuser, it created a rift that caused him to be cut off from important relationships. Unbeknownst to us, they did not have family connections or friends outside of the group. Tad was so transparent sharing the impact the abuse had on him and how God was beginning to heal him, our entire group was in tears.

But something profound happened in addition to Tad's healing. That particular meeting became a "hinge moment" that triggered our group to a new and deeper level of intimacy. Several other members shared difficult personal stories and real healing was taking place. The power of breaking that first secret was enormous.

The irony was that Tad was offered a job with benefits outside of the area. At their farewell they tearfully said that for the first time they found a family but they were being called away from it. We assured them that the Lord had His people strategically placed all over.

Personal Attention: Wanderers

When I was a boy, someone showed me an old Victrola record player and put a heavy black 78-rpm album on to show me how it worked. Accompanied by lots of static, a woman's warbly voice sang sadly, "Where is my wandering boy tonight, the boy of my tenderest care?" Why that maudlin song has stuck in my head all these years, I have no idea. I have since learned that the song was written by a very well-known hymn writer of the nineteenth century, Robert Lowry. The song appeared in hymnals because, I suppose, there are always Christian parents in any church who worry about a prodigal child.

Our church family should be more aware of our wanderers, too. James 5:19–20 says, "My brothers and sisters, if one of you should wander from the truth and someone should bring that person back, remember this: Whoever turns a sinner from the error of their way will save them from death and cover over a multitude of sins." Wanderers require personal work. You can't start a program for that.

Pastors tend to give a lot more time to trying to get new sheep than in taking care of those God has given us. In Ezekiel 34:4–6, God condemned Israel's shepherds: "You have not strengthened the weak or healed the sick or bound up the injured. You have not brought back the strays or searched for the lost. . . . My sheep wandered over all the mountains and on every high hill. They were scattered over the whole earth, and no one searched or looked for them." How many pastors give little or no thought to those who are spiritually sick or injured, or who have strayed far from God's flock?

The larger our church grows, the harder it is to keep track of people who slip away quietly.

The larger our church grows, the harder it is to keep track of people who slip away quietly, like a teenager sneaking out their bedroom window. Since I preached on those verses in James, I've become more diligent about pursuing the wanderers.

Personal Attention: Pastors' Prayers

For many people, there is nothing quite like having their pastor pray for them. We fulfill a kind of priestly function for them, and it is a high privilege. I was talking with a veteran pastor about pastoral counseling. He said, "I think the most important thing I ever did for my people was to pray with them." That brings me to this story of one of the most remarkable things that has ever happened to me in the ministry.

In the spring of 2015, God distinctly prompted me to try something that I'd never done before, never even heard of. During Lent, the six weeks leading up to Easter, I felt God wanted me to pray for a half-hour with every household in my church. It seemed like an outlandish idea to me. I mean, who can meet with so many people! But I created lots of spaces on my calendar and issued the invitation. To my surprise, almost every household in the church signed up. Sometimes people came to my office at church. Other times I'd go to a particular community for the evening to visit homes. I could make three half hour visits per night, fifteen minutes apart for travel.

I told folks we weren't going to chat. No refreshments. No tours of the house. Kids were welcome and usually came. Each time I told them I had asked God to help me "pray for what he wanted to give and listen to what he wants to say." Before we started, I made note of their prayer requests. I told them they didn't have to do anything; just receive. I said that part of the time we'd be quiet, and that I'd try not to pray till I sensed Jesus prompting me to. I began each time by saying, "Lord, you tell us that your sheep know your voice, so we are listening."

In the silence, I tried to relax inwardly and be aware of what the Lord brought to the front of my mind about these people who are so dear to Him and to me. I know these people. They are my flock. So I thought of their quiet strengths and things that I love about them, what they've been through and ways they bless others around them. I also remembered personal struggles that few other people knew about. I assumed that what I love about them, Jesus loves about them, only more. So I might pray, "Jennie, the Lord sees how faithfully you've cared for our church's children. You are kind, you love them for Jesus' sake, and you are an honor to His name." Or perhaps I'd pray for someone, "Your life has been so stressful lately. Lord Jesus, my friends here are weary. Thank You that they have remained faithful to You. Please quiet their hearts and bring rest to their souls."

The quiet moments seemed almost as important as what I said. I resolved to be succinct in what I said so there was time for silence. A sense of peace seemed to settle as the minutes passed. One woman told me she felt as though she'd been held by Jesus.

It was like surprising people with flowers in Jesus' name.

I thought this would be draining work. It wasn't. It was like surprising people with flowers in Jesus' name. More than one person said, "No one has ever prayed for me like this before." By the time I finished at Easter I had prayed with ninety-six households and 195 people.

I prayed with one dear couple in their home. Barb's fear of the future hung heavy in the air. We sat quietly together while I tried to listen for the Lord's direction, for what He wanted me to say or pray. I was surprised when the words came: "All will be well. All will be well." It was as if fresh air filled the room with relief. A few minutes later, when our time ended, Barb said, "I know Jesus is always with us, but tonight . . . He was right here in this room!"

To consider:

What are ways your church is good at personal attention? Who are especially effective at this kind of ministry?

Are there people who have drifted away from your church whom God might want you to pursue?

9

What Care Looks Like

Families take care of each other, even when it's a hassle. Older kids babysit when they'd rather be on their own. Mom rocks the crying child at 2:00 a.m. Dad gives up his softball league to coach his kid's Little League. A man drives two hours to visit his aging aunt. Church families are no different. Caring for our brothers and sisters is a test of our family commitment. It's pretty easy on Sunday mornings to sing out the songs we love. But when someone has had a death in the family, will their brothers and sisters bring meals? Will there be someone to help a single woman move to a new apartment? Are people praying for the person who can't find a job?

I was a new solo pastor, still trying to get to know the people in our congregation, when I realized that I hadn't seen a certain couple since shortly after I arrived. Through the grapevine I learned that the man had lost his job several months before. We lived near Pittsburgh and the steel mills were closing right and left, so that was no surprise. I learned that since no one had called on them, they'd left the church.

My first reaction was, *how was I supposed to know this?!* Which was a valid point. They *could* have called. But I learned a valuable lesson. People leave if we don't take care of them in times of trouble. In times of significant suffering, people often withdraw. They are wary of sympathy. They may keep their distance from their church family. But a pastor who reaches out to them can bring Jesus' own touch if we're gentle and patient. And a church that doesn't show care leaves their back door standing open.

Caring for individuals is challenging for a church focused on growth because care saps a congregation's energy and resources. After all, we only have so much energy. Caring for our church family may not help our church grow bigger, but it will help our church grow more like Christ. In a striking example of inefficiency, the good shepherd goes after the one lost sheep.

God graces every church with some people who are spiritually gifted for mercy and helping, an indication of how important these ministries are to the Lord. Such people have a God-given instinct about the burdens of their brothers and sisters, the way some musicians have perfect pitch. When our son was an infant my wife slipped on some icy steps while carrying him. He was okay but she was badly bruised and traumatized. My low capacity for sympathy was quickly evident, despite my sincere efforts to care for her. Then Diane came over. She brought soup. She stood by Susan's bedside, listening and empathizing. Then she prayed. I watched from the doorway thinking, "Who's the pastor around here!"

Not long ago in my Sunday morning prayer I prayed for a needy family facing a medical crisis. After the service, someone pressed a generous check for them into my hand and on the way home I got a text from a brother who was thinking through how we could create a quick response team for such situations. These are gifts of helps.

Such gifted people lead the rest of us, not only in the acts of mercy and help, but in the attitudes from which we can all learn. Like me watching Diane, the church watches those whose hearts are touched by emergencies, sorrows, and needs. Mercy means they don't worry too much about who deserves help. They make us all more tender.

In chapter 3, I mentioned our friend Anne Tohme, who, along with her husband Kelvin, has taught her children that they have two families, one named Tohme and the other named Christian. Anne has given a great deal of thought to the way a church cares for people because she's struggled with a debilitating illness where her body does not properly absorb nourishment. It has been a grueling ordeal and there is no clear end in sight. Our church has cared for her. I remember one Sunday when her illness was at its worst. I addressed her from the pulpit before I prayed. "Anne, we want you to know that there will never be a day—and rarely even an hour—when someone in this church won't be praying for you." Anne remembers that. She says, "It has carried me on hard days, knowing that people are praying for me."

Anne collaborated with me on this chapter. You'll remember that she had picked up on the idea from Ryan Kwon of a "family win." Carrying one another's burdens, even when it is draining for the church, is a family win. When a congregation understands that we're a family, we will care for one another in extraordinary ways.

God's Comfort through Community

Second Corinthians 1:3–4 begins, "Praise be to the God and Father of our Lord Jesus Christ, the Father of compassion and the God of all comfort . . ." The Father's mercies are all the component parts of salvation. The comfort of God is a deep, "it is well with my soul" assurance. Paul had suffered greatly. His character and churches had been assaulted. His body was attacked and his heart was broken. The comfort Paul needed was not a cozy chair with a hot drink and a good book. Paul needed soul comfort, the comfort that says, *I have a God who is in control and who has come for me. I have a God who takes away my sins and provides me with eternal life. I have a God who promises never to leave me or forsake me, because He knows the worst suffering of all and He has overcome. I know He can help me to overcome and will bring me to glory with Him one day. Praise be to the God of mercies and the God of all comfort.*

Paul continues, "who *comforts* us in all our troubles." The word translated comfort, *parakleseos*, is related to Jesus' description of the Holy Spirit as the *parakletos*, the Comforter. It is a compound word made from *to the side of + to call*. Thus, the Lord's presence by our side is our comfort. God's comfort is not always of the motherly "there, there, everything will be all right" variety. He may encourage us like a coach urging players to push through fatigue, or a doctor patiently explaining the needed treatment, or a lawyer who promises to be our advocate. He may sit with us silently in grief. Whatever form God's comfort takes we have the assurance of Scripture that in times of trouble God is by our side. A long time ago, in a season of distress, I (Lee) wrote a little song. The verse described the importance of God's mighty power and name. The chorus said,

> "But Lord, tonight I need a father to walk with me awhile,
>   To nod your head and say you understand,
> To put your arm around my trembling shoulders as we walk,
>   And tell me that you love me as I am."

I (Anne) have learned that a lot of what I used to think about God's comfort has been stripped away. His comfort does not mean that our situation will get better or that our troubles will disappear. In fact, things may get worse. There is no promise of healing, a good job, a baby, mar-

Scripture promises that God will never leave us, not that we will never *feel* alone.

riage, or the depression lifting. We aren't even assured of the *sense* of God's presence. Scripture only promises that He will never leave us, not that we will never *feel* alone.

Paul brings this message of comfort home: "who comforts us in all our troubles, *so that we can comfort those in any trouble with the comfort we ourselves receive from God.*" Comfort is a family matter. God doesn't dispense His comfort by Himself. He invests His comfort in His people, to be invested in others like the talents in Jesus' parable. We are intended to be a family of comforters. Those in our congregation who have trusted and obeyed God in their hardships are more valuable to our church than we realize. They understand better than others how the mercies of God fortify and befriend fellow believers in "all our troubles."

Alexander Maclaren said, "The worst of all sorrows is a

wasted sorrow." When I (Lee) was a young pastor, I watched a woman in our church suffering from multiple sclerosis. I knew that God has His purposes in our suffering, but it seemed like she endured a lot of pain for a small payoff. But as I considered this, I concluded that God is too good to ever waste an ounce of our suffering. I realized that God maximized her suffering by training me and many others in our church family for our own times of trouble. We all saw her faithful perseverance in Christ and we realized (perhaps subconsciously), "If she can be faithful, I can be faithful." Her suffering strengthened us all, assuring us that God would help us as He did her.

In March 2017, I (Anne) was hospitalized and our church family started organizing meals for us. Over a year later they were still bringing meals. I am so weary of this health situation but our brothers and sisters aren't, and their perseverance helps me keep going. The food they brought was a tremendous blessing to us, but do you know what has meant the most to me? That twice a week someone from church came to our home to bring food, a hug, and an encouraging word or a prayer. Knowing I am not alone in the struggle strengthens me. Does anyone care? Yes! They do.

On our refrigerator is a verse that came home from our kids' Sunday school class one day, Proverbs 11:25, "A generous person will prosper; whoever refreshes others will be refreshed." A church family grows more Christlike when they practice that proverb. When I thanked those who've brought us meals, they would often respond, "It's my pleasure." I thought they were just being nice. Then I started signing up myself to bring meals to others. It's so fun! Even though I am exhausted and going through my own struggles, I find it so refreshing to find ways to care for other people. And now I respond in the same way: "It is truly my pleasure!"

Caring for our church family is practical: wedding and baby showers, funeral luncheons, meals for the sick or those who have newborns, visits to shut-ins, rides and help with housework. Our Care Team leader said to me, "Anne, little things make such a big difference. None of these things are hard, but they go a long way to showing love." These little things acknowledge someone's situation and that they are not alone in it. Doing this may be all we can offer but sometimes it is enough to keep someone going.

In December our Care Team makes stacks of Christmas cards available for people to write in for our shut-ins, and we provide big white mailboxes to hold the cards. Cindy was delivering those Christmas cards to Maureen, whose Parkinson's disease keeps her housebound. Maureen was moved and said, "Even though I am not present physically, my church has never forgotten me." Recently I (Anne) received a surprise flower delivery—from Maureen, caring for me. She may not be with us, but she is very much a part of our family.

So many church families love one another in ways like this. Countless churches, large and small, have stories of these ministries. When we care for one another, the word gets around, just as Jesus said it would in John 13:35, "By this everyone will know that you are my disciples, if you love one another." People are blown away when I tell them that my church has been supporting our family with meals for over a year. They can't comprehend that type of long-haul sacrificial love. It becomes an opportunity for me to talk about how "we love because he first loved us." It provides a chance to share the gospel of Christ.

Covering Each Other

I (Anne) have a dear friend who was going through a difficult and confusing season. We were talking about how we were doing. I told her, "Friend, I am praying for you, fervently and faithfully. I believe that God is going to show up for you." Then I quipped, "I can't seem to find the faith to pray that for myself, but I sure can for you." She said to me, "Good, because I can't pray for myself anymore either, but I have faith and prayer for you, Anne. We can cover each other!"

The people in our churches don't need to pray for *everyone's* needs, but they should pray for *someone's* needs.

There's an old motto: "The family that prays together stays together." That fits the church family. Our prayers for brothers and sisters facing heavy pressures bind us together in love. How we communicate prayer needs for one another varies from church to church. Some churches, especially as they get larger, struggle to find workable systems for engaging people in intercessory prayer. The people in our churches don't need to pray for *everyone's* needs, but they should pray for *someone's* needs.

At our church size, we can use email blasts to reach almost everyone. We send urgent requests for people in our church family to everyone on our list because it is everyone's responsibility to pray. We seek volunteers for a second list, Uplift Prayer, who receive requests for specific concerns that extend beyond our church family (close relatives, for example). When we send out a prayer request about someone in the church we try to include their photo to help people put a face with the name. We also often include their address and encourage our people to send them cards, which they do.

Burdened brothers or sisters are encouraged just to know people pray for them, of course, but our prayers are more than spiritual Hallmark cards. We are laying hold of God's help. Sometimes people think that the more people they can have praying, the better. I don't see that idea in Scripture. But it is clear that we are to seek the prayers of others. Jesus did so, as did Paul. Again and again, I've been told how sufferers have felt the uplift of God as people prayed for them.

Those who are sick are also told in Scripture that they can call on the elders of the church to pray for them. Again, this is family business. Christian friends should certainly pray for one another but it is also important to "call the elders of the church." James 5:14–15 says, "Is anyone among you sick? Let them call the elders of the church to pray over them and anoint them with oil in the name of the LORD. And the prayer offered in faith will make the sick person well; the LORD will raise them up. If they have sinned, they will be forgiven."

The Greek word translated here as *make well* is often translated elsewhere as *save*. In fact, the word is used only a few verses later in the expression, "will *save* them from death" (v. 20). Do you see how this language, in another context, would sound like the gospel? *Prayer of faith, save, raise up, sins forgiven.* James does that on purpose. Praying for physical or mental healing draws on gospel realities. Sometimes a sick heart infects the body and other times a sick body or mind infects the heart. In either case we need God's healing. We call the elders for several reasons: they represent the church family, they are wise in God's Word, they love their flock for Jesus' sake, and they believe that God can and will heal what is most desperately diseased or dysfunctional within a believer by the power of Jesus.

Speaking as one who suffers, I (Anne) feel that of all the good things we can pray for our brothers and sisters in trouble, nothing may be more important than God's peace. We often pray for miraculous healings (and we should), but when God's peace blankets

When God's peace blankets someone's heart in hard times, that too is miraculous.

someone's heart in hard times, that too is miraculous. People marvel at such peace where they never expect to see it. I pray Philippians 4:6 for myself and for others: "And the peace of God, which transcends all understanding, will guard your hearts and your minds in Christ Jesus." I pray Jesus' promise in John 14:27, "Peace I leave with you; my peace I give you. I do not give to you as the world gives. Do not let your hearts be troubled and do not be afraid."

"Rejoice with Those Who Rejoice"

We might overlook the care we show when we celebrate with others in our church. Romans 12:15 says, "Rejoice with those who rejoice." When one of our elders, Ric, was moving away we asked if he had any counsel for us. The first thing he said was, "Celebrate more."

I (Lee) still remember visiting a large church a long time ago when the pastor identified a couple celebrating their fiftieth wedding anniversary. He talked about their example and thanked them for being a model for the church. Everyone gave them a standing ovation. Take time to cheer for graduates, new babies, and newlyweds. Celebrate new Christians. We give standing ovations to our missionaries when they visit us because I want our people to see them as our champions. Write cards (not just emails) of congratulations. Honor those whose service deserves honor.

I (Anne) remember being new to the church and pregnant with our daughter, Lauryn. Jennifer, a young woman at church, told me that she wanted to throw a baby shower for me. I was nervous about this because I was new. I even told her, "Jennifer, I don't think anyone will come." I was wrong. A roomful of women, some of whom I didn't even know, came to the shower to celebrate Lauryn and me. That memory will stay with me forever. I felt so cared for by our church, to think that people who hardly knew me would go out of their way to rejoice with me.

When someone's big moments are missed, we're telling them that they aren't seen, or that such personal accomplishments don't matter in our church family. Church leaders can create a climate where we rejoice with those who rejoice if we seek out the joys within our church family. Not long ago, Wongto, Tiala, and their son, Hanglen, all originally from northeastern India, became US citizens. We cheered for that too.

"Visiting the Sick without a Thought as to the Danger"

In his book, *When the Church Was a Family,* Joseph Hellerman retells a story first told by Eusebius in his history of the church. Hellerman writes, "Around AD 260, a devastating plague afflicted the great city of Alexandria. People were dying right and left, and the church family suffered some devastating losses. The response of the local church to the plague constitutes one of the most powerful examples of Christian brotherhood in the annals of church history." Dionysius, the overseer of the Christian community in the city, wrote of the extraordinary risks and losses suffered by the church in caring for the sick and dying. Christians were:

> visiting the sick without a thought as to the danger, assiduously
> ministering to them, tending them in Christ, and so most gladly
> departed this life along with them; being infected with the
> disease from others, drawing upon themselves the sickness from
> their neighbors, and willingly taking over their pains. . . . In this
> manner the best . . . of our brethren departed this life. [1]

To consider:

How have you seen care for your people help your church mature in Christ? How does that work?

How could you more effectively enlist prayer for those carrying heavy burdens?

10

The Whole
Church Preaches

Richard Wagamese was a celebrated Ojibwe writer from Canada. He came from a terrible background. He described his first home as a tent hung from a spruce bough. According to an article by Susan Walker in the *Literary Review of Canada*,

> In February 1958, when he was not yet three, Wagamese and his three siblings were abandoned in a bush camp when the adults left on a drinking binge in Kenora. When the food and firewood ran out, his elder sister hauled the children across a frozen bay by sled. They were found by a provincial policeman, huddled next to an old railroad depot. Placed in foster care, Wagamese entered into an equally perilous life that removed him from his family and community for 21 years. Beatings and abuse in foster care led to his leaving home at 16, to live on the street, in and out of prison, abusing drugs and alcohol. He was a lost soul at 25 when his brother Charles located him.[1]

In his collection of short and true stories, *One Native Life*, Wagamese tells about his boyhood friend Shane Rivers.

Shane's family was very poor—bare cupboards, empty refrigerator, curling linoleum floors, and no TV. But Richard loved going to Shane's home nonetheless. He explains why.

> Shane's family gathered around their wood stove for meals, suppers of cabbage soup with dumplings, Wonder Bread and margarine, and the talk they shared was different from the talk around our family table. Mr. and Mrs. Rivers took time to ask each of their five kids about their day. They asked more questions about what they heard, and the meal passed with everyone being listened to and looked at—even me. . . .
>
> I'd look back at that worn old house from the end of the driveway and think it was the warmest place I'd ever been . . .
>
> . . . I'd have given anything as a kid for half the heart that was shared around their fire. I'd have given anything to be heard, seen and validated every day of my life.[2]

What a beautiful metaphor for the church!

Sometimes when I talk about the church as home, friends are concerned that thinking about church this way will minimize the importance of outreach and evangelism. Won't we get too ingrown, thinking about ourselves all the time? Frankly, that's a danger for churches no matter how they see themselves. But actually it is no more likely that a healthy church-home would be unconcerned about the unsaved than a healthy Christian family on your street would be uninterested in their neighbors. I saw a Christian couple post news on Facebook of the house God provided for them. She wrote, "We asked the Lord to give us HIS house from which we could shine HIS light as a family." The same desire works from a church-home. In both cases we must stir up our love for outsiders but the healthy home is the best kind of home base to reach out to others.

This home-church philosophy of ministry supports any kind of outreach approach. My goal here is not to provide a particular model of evangelism but to make the case that a church-home is always the best base of operations for outreach. There are many books, seminars, and blogs that can help you find the approach best suited to your church family.

The Whole Church Preaches: When Kim Came to Christ

As Joseph Hellerman points out, we put such an emphasis on personal evangelism that we forget how crucial the body of Christ is—all of us together—in spreading the gospel. He writes, "People did not convert to Christianity solely because of what the early Christians believed. They converted because of the way in which the early Christians behaved."[3] By that, he means how they behaved *together*.

Jim and Evy first met Kim when Kim was giving out food samples at a store. They struck up a friendship. Kim was most definitely *not* a Christian. She defiantly regarded herself as an angry atheist. But Jim and Evy had her to their home and invited her to ride with them to church. She came but she was locked and loaded, ready for combat! In their Sunday school class, she dominated with her questions. Some were honest. Some were just skeptical. I remember sitting with her at a party where she insisted that heaven held no appeal for her.

Gradually, she warmed up. She moved from angry atheist to agnostic. Her questions just kept on coming. Slowly her defenses wore down. It wasn't just that her questions were answered. It was being around Christians, seeing our love for one another and for her. She liked the life of the church family and we liked her spunk and smile. She became an usher. Meanwhile, God kept dropping little signs along her way— things that wouldn't have meant much to me but to her were divine messages.

When we formed a choir to sing on Good Friday and Easter, Kim joined. As we rehearsed each week, she was internalizing the messages of the songs. The choir met early on Good Friday evening to go over our music one more time. After we'd rehearsed, our director pointed at Jim in the back row and asked if he'd lead us in prayer. But when she pointed at Jim, *Kim*, who was one row in front of him, thought *she'd* been invited to pray. "I'd love to," she said. People in the choir glanced at one another sideways.

Then Kim prayed. She thanked God for the gift of His Son, and for the sacrifice Jesus made on the cross for us as sinners. She said how wonderful that was, and how much God must love us. After she said Amen, a few of us wondered if God had heard what we had! A few minutes later, I caught up with Kim and said, "Your prayer sounded like a Christian praying." She looked at me, paused, and said with surprise, "I guess I am." Somehow, there, on Good Friday, in her prayer with us all listening, Kim trusted Christ. A few minutes later she was telling others what had happened to her.

No *one* led Kim to Christ. We *all* led Kim to Christ. Our whole church preached, as did a couple of Christians from other churches.

"Fighting Flesh and Living in the Spirit"

I grew up hearing the old evangelism adage "each one reach one." I've never heard of that actually working. It should be more like "all of us, together, reach one." Our church family not only provides the healthy environment from which we go out to the world, but we also are one preacher, collectively proclaiming Christ, in sync with other churches.

That is how it worked when the church began. Acts 2:42–47 says,

> They devoted themselves to the apostles' teaching and to fellowship, to the breaking of bread and to prayer. Everyone was filled with awe at the many wonders and signs performed by the apostles. All the believers were together and had everything in common. They sold property and possessions to give to anyone who had need. Every day they continued to meet together in the temple courts. They broke bread in their homes and ate together with glad and sincere hearts, praising God and enjoying the favor of all the people. And the Lord added to their number daily those who were being saved.

Christian community *is* evangelistic by nature, not only in declaration of the gospel but in our life together. Mark Sayers, in his book *Strange Days: Life in the Spirit in a Time of Upheaval*, quotes Lesslie Newbigin: "Such a community is the primary hermeneutic of the gospel," for "all the statistical evidence goes to show that those within our secularized societies who are being drawn out of unbelief to faith in Christ say that they were drawn *through the friendship of a local congregation*." Sayers adds, "Just as the temple [in the Old Testament era] was the magnet people were drawn to, the life of the Spirit lived in the temple 'of a collective body' becomes magnetic itself."[4]

He also says, "Christians, formed by the church, shaped by its relational rhythms, abiding with Christ, fighting flesh and living in the Spirit, are built for the real world."[5]

In his first epistle, Peter portrays the life of the church in an often-hostile culture, not unlike our own. He writes in 1 Peter 2:11–12, "Dear friends, I urge you, as foreigners and exiles, to abstain from sinful desires, which wage war against your soul. Live such good lives among the pagans that, though they accuse you of doing wrong, they may see your good deeds and glorify God on the day he visits us."

Some communities are not ripe for harvest. Not all fields are. Peter's pre-evangelism prescription was a church family whose good lives, taken together and publicly evident, pointed undeniably to God and silenced the malicious accusations of their neighbors.

I spoke with a friend who pastors a rural church. He told me that there has long been a pernicious rumor in that community about their congregation. The church has been there nearly 125 years! It has never had a wisp of unorthodox teaching. Yet when a couple told their family where they'd started attending, the reply was, "Isn't that a cult?" Short of going from farmhouse to farmhouse, the only way that church can mute such gossip is by their consistently godly lives together.

Patio Fishing

The picture in the *Chicago Tribune* showed five adults seated in a relaxed circle on a small flagstone patio under shade trees near a suburban street, a little wrought-iron table in the middle. A couple of kids were there, too, and a dog sleeping under one chair. Barbara Brotman, the writer of the column, said, "It would have been charming, but unremarkable, if it had been in their backyard, the usual spot for patios, but this patio was in their front yard."

One of her neighbors, Steve, had put the patio in the front yard, right along his driveway, so he could keep an eye on his kids. "It looked so inviting," wrote Brotman, "especially when Steve had a bottle of wine and a stack of plastic cups. Or when he set out a fire pit and built a bonfire. So people began to wander over, sit down, and talk. It was so easy and low-key. No invitation required; if you saw people out there, you joined them. Which couldn't make Steve—a gregarious sort who refers to his patio-sitting as 'fishing for people'—happier." He calls his little patio "the Conversation Curve." The article was titled, "Front Patio Makes a Great Hook if Fishing for People."[6] (If there was ever a headline to make a preacher sit up and pay attention, that was it!)

A year later, almost to the day, Brotman wrote a follow-up article describing how Steve's idea had caught on. One of her readers, a community leader in Hammond, Indiana, was inspired by her article to get funding to promote "micro parks" in homeowners' front yards. According to her column, at the official unveiling ceremony, "Rev. Stephen Gibson, whose St. Mary's Church has two benches of its own . . . gave a benediction. 'I ask God to bless this bench as a symbol of the spirit of welcome,' he said."[7]

Maybe your church property would lend itself to a micro park, but think of this as a metaphor. It's not the benches and table that made Steve's idea work. It was *him*, sitting out there in his Conversation Curve where he could greet his neighbors, fishing for people. The security and health of a church-home prepares believers to do that—to fish for people.

After I read those columns, I moved from sitting on our back patio to our front porch and have since made friends with all the kids and most of their parents in the houses around us. I've taken some of the kids Christmas caroling the last three years, and we had them and their parents in for cocoa and cookies afterward. I hang out regularly at Einstein Bros. Bagels in the morning so I can develop friendships. If I'm going to meet with someone from church, I often suggest we meet there. Sometimes my Einstein friends meet my church friends.

Late one Friday afternoon, I was in my office working on my sermon, the window open to the breeze. Three boys rode their bikes into our parking lot and circled a couple times. Then they pulled up right outside our front door to talk. They couldn't see me but I could see and hear them. I saw one boy peer through the door and then say to his friends, "You know, I don't think I've ever been in a church in my whole life." I was stunned. An utterly unchurched kid five feet from our door! But by the time I got to the door, they were gone. How many others in the neighborhood are like that, I wondered?

Whenever I get the chance, I tell unchurched people about the life of our church family. If they won't come in, maybe I can help them look through the window.

Whenever I get the chance, I tell unchurched people about the life of our church family. If they won't come in, maybe I can help them look through the window. I tell them how we enjoy and pray for each other, about answers to prayer or ways people have loved each other, about how generous and non-judgmental my brothers and sisters are, or how we struggle to know what Jesus would have us think about the same national issues we are all grappling with.

In his book *The Connecting Church*, Randy Frazee builds a powerful case for the wide-ranging benefits of authentic small group communities. For example, one group of five house-holds in the same neighborhood started their own version of front-yard patio living. They prayed and provided meals for a neighborhood family whose wife/mother was dealing with cancer. They provided a monthly birthday party for residents of a local assisted-living center. They help provide backpacks and school supplies for a local Christian charity. They joined a ministry at church together.[8]

There is nothing else in the world like a good church home. Whenever you can, move your life together out of the build-ing and out to the front patio.

Storm Homes

I grew up in a small farming community near the South Dakota–North Dakota border. Winter weather there can quickly turn nasty. Sometimes when a blizzard would blow up during the day, the farm kids would get stranded in town because it wasn't safe for the buses to take them home over snow-drifted roads. The school made arrangements with families in town to be "storm homes" when that happened. The farm parents knew that if their child couldn't come home on the bus, a certain family in town would care for their child that night. Not long ago, when I was home visiting the church I grew up in, Roger said, "Your home was my storm home when I was in school." The important thing with our storm homes was not merely safe shelter. It was having a family—a home away from home—for those stranded kids.

That's another metaphor for the church—a storm home. There are so many people who don't have a safe home for their hearts. "When [Jesus] saw the crowds, he had compassion on them, because they were harassed and helpless, like sheep without a shepherd." Then He told His disciples, "Ask the Lord of the harvest, therefore, to send out workers into his harvest field" (Matt. 9:36–38). In answer to those prayers God, in His great mercy (and sometimes without our knowledge), assigns certain spiritually homeless people to our church so we can be their storm home. They may come to our church service or simply find themselves in the company of a few members of our church family. They not only meet us; they also meet Jesus, because wherever His people gather, Jesus is there, too. When God's household loves one another, there is no place better, no place safer, for a storm-tossed soul than among us. Remember that line from Psalm 68:6, "God sets the lonely in families."

Loneliness is one of the great afflictions of our time, and Christians are not exempt. Trouble is, hiding a lonely soul is pretty easy. That's the challenge to drawing people into the family. I know of no way to discern who they are except to ask the Lord to make such people evident to us. There are times when I sense an impulse to probe a little with someone, "You've been on my mind lately. How are you doing? Would you like to get together for a cup of coffee?" I've also asked others, "Would you look for a chance to check on 'Kathy'? I have a hunch she needs some attention."

One of our church's stories happened before my time. In the late '80s, a man named Jim showed up at Village Church. No one knows how he found his way to us. He was a Vietnam vet, wounded in mind and heart, who lived alone in near-poverty in a trailer. He drank too much and didn't take very good care of himself. In fact, because of his drinking and all, he was puffy and bloated, and not very appealing. But he showed up in church. And that posed a problem, of course, because he made folks uncomfortable.

But the pastor at the time—another Pastor Lee—welcomed him. That Pastor Lee and his wife, Joyce, often had Jim to dinner. So did Don and Nancy and others. Jim became a Christian. Don gave him a Bible. Jim would come and just sit alone in the sanctuary because he felt peaceful. He sat around a church campfire one night till 3:00 a.m., listening in amazement to Christians tell their stories.

Jim volunteered to cut the church's grass and take care of the flowers. Problem was, he would do it on Sunday morning before church, and then come into church in his cut-offs, smelling of alcohol and grass and gasoline. He was a challenge, and he never really got his life all put together. But people welcomed him. The congregation became his home.

Jim died about three years later. Don found him in his trailer. And now that humble, blessed brother waits in paradise for his white robe, his family reunion, and the Wedding Supper of the Lamb.

To consider:

How have you seen your whole church preach the gospel?

How could you help your congregation preach better *together*, whether through a program or informally?

11

Parenting the Church Family

I was twenty-two when I went to my first church board meeting. I was a part-time youth pastor and choir director. I can't remember why I had been invited. The main order of business was to establish the budget for the next year, and I certainly had nothing to contribute on that score. All I remember was the treasurer, still in his business suit from work, declaring, "Our giving this year was ____ , so let's add five percent to that." And that was that. In my naiveté, I assumed leaders would talk about the congregation's needs and opportunities and that they'd pray together before making decisions. Instead, it seemed that the budget was established by a five-percent-more business formula. I was disillusioned.

In over forty years as a church leader, I've been to a lot of board and committee meetings since then! I've realized that it is easy for church leaders to think that their job is all about the meetings.

If we think of the church primarily as an organization

rather than a family, we will consistently think of leadership in organizational terms. We will draw our language from business books and evaluate our success by metrics. But as I said in chapter 1, if we think of our church primarily as a family, then our approach to leadership will shift. Families don't usually think of themselves in terms of metrics.

The church *is* an organization, of course. The early church had to deal with organizational issues as all congregations have had to. Acts 6 tells how the apostles, along with the whole church, delegated the daily distribution of food to seven men who were "full of the Holy Spirit and wisdom." In 2 Corinthians 8–9 Paul gave specific instructions for the management of funds for the poor in Jerusalem. Paul says in Romans 12:8 that leading "diligently" is one of the spiritual gifts. He gave instructions in the Pastoral Epistles for appointing elders and deacons, as well as how to manage other church issues.

Peter told elders, "Be shepherds of God's flock that is under your care" (1 Peter 5:2), which requires us to feed, lead, and guard the flock. Many leaders focus on the organizational aspects of those assignments, but they are primarily *relational* tasks. In Paul's first letter to Timothy he explained why he was writing: "If I am delayed, you will know how people ought to conduct themselves in God's household, which is the church of the living God, the pillar and foundation of the truth" (1 Tim. 3:15). He meant their behavior, not their goal-setting abilities. In 1 Thessalonians 2:7–12, Paul said he had been like a nursing mother and like a father to

The work of a shepherd and a parent are much alike—to lead, feed, and guard.

them. The work of a shepherd and a parent are much alike—to lead, feed, and guard.

In an article entitled "From Relevant Dude to Spiritual Father," Kevin Miller wrote,

> I've been experimenting at church with "Transformation Conversations," extended times of listening to another man and then helping him form a spiritual-growth plan for the coming year. (Mature women are beginning to do the same with younger women.) It generally takes two 90-minute conversations before I feel I know the shape of someone's soul well enough to offer a few "pastoral invitations."
>
> In one recent Transformation Conversation, we talked honestly about this young man's vocation, money, relationships, marriage. We finished, and he said, "Since my wife and I attend worship regularly, serve, and give, it would be easy to conclude we're doing fine. But I need shepherding, too. And I don't think I felt fully shepherded until right now."[1]

Pastors and Elders as Parents

There's not much difference, spiritually speaking, between a shepherd and a parent. Parenting, though, is a more relational role. Stephen L. Woodworth identifies three roles of fathers in the New Testament world: (1) bestow identity, (2) teach, and (3) provide a model. Paul portrays himself as a father to each of the churches he planted, and he speaks of fulfilling these three roles for them.[2] It stands to reason that these are roles that pastors and elders should fill as well. This is usually *how* leaders lead best—as spiritual parents.

Many pastors feel the responsibility of these roles—bestowing identity, teaching, and providing a model—more than their elders do. I believe that those roles are part of what we sometimes call a shepherd's heart. Elders are often recruited for administrative leadership—to be on the Elder Board, i.e., to handle the business of the church. In our church, when it is time to seek nominees for our Board of Elders, I like to have a personal conversation with each person considering the role. I've realized how often I emphasize to these people the dynamics and duties of our *board*, but I haven't sufficiently emphasized this shepherding role, this parental approach to our congregation. But unless the elders own this part of their responsibility, all the relational leadership of the church family falls back on pastors.

Look more closely at 1 Thessalonians 2:7–8 (ESV):

> But we were gentle among you, *like a nursing mother* taking care of her own children. So, being affectionately desirous of you, we were ready to share with you not only the gospel of God but also our own selves, because you had become very dear to us.

A nursing mother is careful, soft, gentle. She makes sure the infant is nourished. We especially need to be this way with new Christians. They don't know how to feed themselves, how to behave or stand on their own. We can't be guilty of shaking babies! We feed them not only the mother's milk of the gospel, but the example of the gospel lived out in our very lives. That requires close relationships, authenticity, and vulnerability.

Recently I saw one of our elders in the foyer after a service, alone in a corner with a woman who was facing a terribly difficult situation. He asked thoughtful questions and helped her think through some of her tough decisions. He looked for ways we could help and he prayed with her. He was "like a nursing mother."

Paul continued in verses 10–12: "You are witnesses, and so is God, of how holy, righteous and blameless we were among you who believed. For you know that we dealt with each of you *as a father* deals with his own children, encouraging, comforting and urging you to live lives worthy of God, who calls you into his kingdom and glory."

Two of the fatherly roles noted by Stephen Woodworth are mentioned here: modeling and teaching. We know that elders are described as overseers of the church, but they, too, are being "overseen" by the others in the church family. Church leaders must be *seen* in order to be *heard*—perhaps in their small groups, in service efforts, or simply circulating among the congregation. They don't have to be extroverted, but somewhere in church life, at least some of God's people must be able to observe their godly lives.

Furthermore, we must step into the fatherly role of speaking wisely into the lives of our church family, "encouraging, comforting and urging you to live lives worthy of God." There's something about the words of a good father that stick with us. I only remember my dad telling me twice, "Finish what you start," both under rather stern circumstances, and it has become a guiding principle of my life. When wise fathers speak, it is often like that. Elders don't realize that they are church parents, nor that when they speak to someone—lovingly, wisely, encouragingly—their words carry more weight than they realize. I believe God Himself adds authority and heft to what we say to others for His sake.

If your leadership doesn't know how to approach these

roles, give them a list of all your attendees, ask them to pray for discernment, and then select three or four people or households, outside of those they are already close to. What does God impress upon them as they pray for these people? A difficult challenge they face? An effective ministry they maintain? Some spiritual hurdle they face? Have them speak or write to the people they've chosen. (If they write, encourage them to use pen and paper rather than email, which is easier for people to dismiss.) They might start, "As elders we've been thinking how we could encourage our brothers and sisters. The Lord has brought you to my mind and I want to tell you . . ." Then next month, do it again, till your leaders gain confidence and realize that this is a God-blessed ministry.

What Does It Mean to "Manage Our Families Well"?

When it comes to seeking out those qualified for church leadership Paul looked for an unexpected credential. He told Timothy, "He must manage his own family well and see that his children obey him, and he must do so in a manner worthy of full respect. (If anyone does not know how to manage his own family, how can he take care of God's church?)" (1 Tim. 3:4–5).

I had long assumed that this meant an elder's family had to be exemplary, the kind of family we all wish we had. But that's not what it says. Let me suggest a very free paraphrase, "Whatever kind of family God gives you, lead it in a godly way. Whether your kids are headstrong or compliant, whether your marriage is heavenly or heavy-laden, whether it is a richer or poorer season, a time of sickness or health, honor and obey the Lord. Do not provoke your children to anger by being overbearing or quick-tempered. Seek to work hand-in-hand with your spouse to train your children in the way they should go. The person who has learned to do those hard things at home will be equipped to lead the church, which is, after all, a family too—*God's* family."

Managing our families well suggests that we foster loving and respectful relationships, that our home has a Christ-ward direction, that we bond our household with our church family, and that we demonstrate an abundance of wise and understanding grace. To manage means the careful exercise of God-given authority while not lording it over those entrusted to our care.

If there was ever a phrase to make a parent's knees weak, it is "see that his children obey him." Easier said than done! We all seek to find some workable combination of authority, psychology, prayer, biblical guidance, and providential intervention. Our little rascals can send us to bed in tears. But evidently what we learn about raising obedient children is necessary to leading God's people, who, as any pastor can tell you, is just as challenging.

I corresponded with a pastor who had a frustrating Sunday morning. He was trying to figure out what he should do about a couple of people who prayed very public imprecatory prayers against politicians they didn't favor. On the same Sunday he found that someone had unplugged and hidden cords necessary to recording the service. Was it a mischievous teenager or a parishioner who wants to sabotage and silence him? Things like that call for parental savvy.

Paul adds, "and he must do so in a manner worthy of full respect." We've all seen parents who manage their households in such a way that their children cower before them, or who press their kids under the thumb of "what people will think." We fear that once those kids are out of the home, they'll run as far from their parents—and Jesus—as they can. However, when we see patience, humor, wisdom, and grace in parents, our respect for them gives us confidence not only in their kids' future but in their leadership of the church.

Steve Brown has said, "Children will run from law, and they'll run from grace. The ones who run from law never come back. But the ones who run from grace always come back. Grace draws its own back home."[3] I don't know that those things are "always" true, but he's certainly got a point. It's pretty much the same with church families. We need leaders who know how to stand for God's truth—His law—but who always embody grace. As I like to say, "Law reveals. Grace heals." It's part of managing a household.

In a similar vein, Paul told Titus, "An elder must be blameless, faithful to his wife, a man whose children believe and are not open to the charge of being wild and disobedient. Since an overseer manages God's household, he must be blameless—not overbearing, not quick-tempered, not given to drunkenness, not violent, not pursuing dishonest gain" (Titus 1:6–7).

I sat in a Deacon Board meeting a long time ago, a rookie to the whole leadership business, when one of the deacons, who was deeply respected, tendered his resignation because his grown daughter was far from Christ. He felt he wasn't measuring up to this text. It didn't seem right to me that he should quit over her choices, but I really didn't know what to think.

Since then I have known many church leaders whose grown kids were not walking with Jesus; some who were very far away indeed. Actually, I wonder if pastors don't face that struggle more often than other believers. But I do *not* think such parents are disqualified from church leadership. Surely Paul was speaking of children still within the home, because no one can assure that our adult children, no matter how well raised, will be devoted to Christ. Jesus' own disciple, Judas, one of those He described as His "little children," abandoned Him.

I think Paul's intention was to say that an elder's children should grow up learning to trust in the Lord from an early age, and that there should be nothing in the leaders' lives or manner with their kids or spouse that undermines that trust, but rather, builds it up. This goes to the way we teach our children Scripture, how we pray together and celebrate God's answers, and how we demonstrate the heart of Father God. Have we made the gospel credible and winsome to our family? That's what is expected. Only God is the potter of our children's clay hearts. Similarly, when our children are under our roof, we are responsible that they are not "wild and disobedient"—undisciplined, in other words. I suspect that the parent who fulfills the next requirements, "not overbearing, not quick-tempered," is likely to raise children who are learning self-control.

Ten years after seminary, my wife and I had a son. It's a toss-up as to which did more to make me an effective pastor. I certainly came to better understand the nuances of law and grace, the prayers of love, and the heart of the prodigal's father. The benefit of our home life for church leadership is not the management principles we learn. What is important to the church is how to parent the people of God with all their temptations, demands, immaturity, heartaches, gifts, and sibling rivalries that come with the territory.

Taking a Home Audit

Every congregation who loves Christ and His Word has characteristics of a family. How could it be otherwise? However, when we test our church life against some of the evidences we should see in God's household, we may be found wanting. My goal in this book has been to draw attention to those "family values" we ought to display in our churches. I believe that sometimes we try too hard to grow unnaturally fast, to target only a certain demographic, or that our failure to deal with relationship messes stymies the family life God intends for us.

Perhaps church leaders should do a home audit to evaluate the quality of God's household under our care. These questions might help your leadership:

- To what degree have we as leaders given thought to the biblical teaching on the church as God's household? How could we improve our understanding?

- What efforts do we make as leaders to exercise our shepherding and parental roles among our congregation?

- In what ways does our congregation demonstrate strong family traits?

- In what ways does our congregation need to improve as a family?

- What percentage of our congregation sees our church family as a vital aspect of their own spiritual life, and that of their own family?

- Do we communicate to new members and new leaders that we consider it important and biblical to see our church as home?

- Is our church hospitable? Are our leaders hospitable?

Score your church, 1–10, on these areas:

____ Our people love one another, even through stresses and conflict.

____ We experience and express the rest Jesus gives our souls through worship, prayer, and attention to the Word of God.

____ We welcome people well, which has been affirmed to us by visitors.

____ New people might well say, "God is really among you," and "these people love one another and me."

____ We make a priority of giving personal attention to our brothers and sisters. We learn names, listen well, and take time.

____ We invest in caring for the needs of people in our church family.

____ Rather than being ingrown, our family environment stirs our desire to share our faith.

Making It Stick

I want our church to get used to speaking of our life together as home—as family—so I use that kind of language often. Language matters. Language helps. Over the door of our auditorium we have the phrase, "You are no longer foreigners and strangers, but . . . members of [God's] household" (Eph. 2:19). I address all-church emails, "Dear brothers and sisters." We asked a graphic designer in our church to create a new logo that captured our emphasis, which she did through homey yet professional hand lettering. We created a three-minute video introduction for our website and for social media in which I include an explanation of our identity as home.

Several years ago our congregation approved our Core Values. We emphasize these with new members as well as with our leadership. Among our values are these statements:

> **We foster a strong sense of identity as God's family—** brothers and sisters, and children of the heavenly Father, who are homesick for heaven.
>
> **We celebrate our different generations and cultures as a family strength**. We embrace the diversity in our congregation and show our respect for one another in the ways we approach worship, leadership, and fellowship.
>
> **The church is the first home for believers, single or married, children and adults**. We orient all our households to their home in the church.
>
> **Each person matters**. We learn names. We pray for people personally, talk to people personally, and think of

our church in terms of unique individuals around whom we build our ministries.

We are sensitive to matters of nurture and spiritual safety.

The church together, as God's holy and grace-giving family, preaches the gospel. *Our commitment to evangelism and compassion grows out of our life together, and in turn, draws unbelievers into our life together. Thus, we emphasize personal, sacrificial, loving relationships with one another in our church family as the way we position ourselves for outreach.*

This emphasis is not the only thing we talk about in our church. The Bible has many other important matters we need to address. But I do return to this theme in one way or another regularly.

"I'm Behind You"

Dr. Larry Crabb wrote of an incident in the church he attended as a young man. It was customary in this church that young men were encouraged to participate in the communion services by praying out loud. Feeling the pressure of expectation, the young Crabb (who had a problem with stuttering) stood to pray. In a terribly confused prayer, he recalls "thanking the Father for hanging on the cross and praising Christ for triumphantly bringing the Spirit from the grave." When he was finished, he vowed he would never again speak or pray out loud in front of a group.

At the end of the service, not wanting to meet any of the

church elders who might feel constrained to correct his theology, Crabb made for the door. Before he could get out, an older man named Jim Dunbar caught him.

Having prepared himself for the anticipated correction, Crabb instead found himself listening to these words: "Larry, there's one thing I want you to know. Whatever you do for the Lord, I'm behind you one thousand percent."

Crabb reflects in his book: "Even as I write these words, my eyes fill with tears. I have yet to tell that story to an audience without at least mildly choking. Those words were life words. They had power. They reached deep into my being."[4]

That is the power of a church father.

To consider:

If you're a parent, how has that role affected your approach to church ministry?

What are a couple of ideas from this chapter you could use to strengthen your leadership's "parenting" abilities in your church?

12

Close to Home

The worst travel experience of my life happened on a stormy night in April 1999. I was to fly home that evening from Minneapolis to Midway Airport in Chicago. An hour's flight. I'll abbreviate the story. The storms in Chicago meant hours of delays. Finally, take off, circle Iowa, low on fuel, back to Minneapolis. Deplane. Wait. Board again and take off. Wild, wing-wobbling landing at Midway. Midnight, squeezed under the airport eaves with scores of other travelers in torrential rain waiting for the one shuttle bus still operating at that hour. An hour later, squeezing soaked and shivering onto the bus to my car in the long-term lot. It wouldn't start. Rrrrr. Rrrrr. Rrrrr. Finally, it chugs for a few seconds and stops. The next time it chugs I nurse it, jerking and bucking, out to the streets and to the tollway. About 2:30 a.m., halfway home, it smoothes out. Now I can't stay awake. Window down, radio blaring, less than a mile to my exit. Then, out of nowhere, the teeth-jarring, tire-flattening pothole. Coast off the tollway at my exit, tire thumping.

At 3 a.m. I call my wife, who had to get our young son out of bed to come get me. The one thing I thought over and over as that horrible evening steamrolled over me was, "I just want to be home!"

People come to church some Sundays feeling pretty much like that.

Christians are, by nature, itinerants and road warriors, footsore and weary for home. It's in our spiritual DNA.

> By faith Abraham, when called to go to a place he would later receive as his inheritance, obeyed and went, even though he did not know where he was going. By faith he made his home in the promised land like a stranger in a foreign country.... For he was looking forward to the city with foundations, whose architect and builder is God.... All these people were still living by faith when they died. They did not receive the things promised; they only saw them and welcomed them from a distance, admitting that they were foreigners and strangers on earth. People who say such things show that they are looking for a country of their own. If they had been thinking of the country they had left, they would have had opportunity to return. Instead, they were longing for a better country—a heavenly one. Therefore God is not ashamed to be called their God, for he has prepared a city for them. (Heb. 11:8–16)

In 1688, a Swiss scholar named Johannes Hofer learned of a man who had moved from Berne to Basel to study and became mysteriously ill. He was sad for a long time and had "a burning fever." He got worse and it looked as if he would die. His doctors decided if there was to be any hope at all, he needed to "be returned to his native land." As soon as the sixty-mile trip began the man was able "to draw breath more freely . . . to show a better tranquility of mind." As they approached his home, "all the symptoms abated to such a great extent they really relaxed all together, and he was restored to his whole sane self before he entered Berne."

Having considered that story, Hofer coined the word *nostalgia,* combining two Greek words, *nostos,* meaning "return home," and *algia,* meaning "pain." He used it to describe a patient whose yearning to return home had actually made him ill. "It was also during the eighteenth century," writes historian Susan J. Matt, "that an English word for the condition, *homesickness,* was coined."[1] It was needed because it was an age when many people were emigrating or pioneering into new regions. They needed that word.

For most people, homesickness looks *back* across miles or years. For believers in Christ, it looks *forward* to eternity. A church-home makes people homesick the way getting together with one's siblings makes us all wish we could return one more time to the family farm or the house on Maple Street, except we Christians dream of days yet to come, not days that will never return, and the home awaiting us will be nothing like any place we have ever seen.

Every church family bears the responsibility to cultivate a forward-facing homesickness, an eager anticipation of Jesus' return and the place He has prepared for us in heaven. Our challenge isn't Christians who have *no* hope. Most are thankful for these promises. Our problem is the many whose hope is vague, ephemeral, or fanciful, who never give their Christian hope much thought.

> **Every church family bears the responsibility to cultivate a forward-facing homesickness.**

That's when believers become so earthly minded they are of no heavenly good.

Our home together now with God's people, both in our church and with believers in other churches, is a kind of staging ground, a temporary camp, like the circled wagons of pioneers heading west across the prairies. I imagine them sitting around the campfire after the kids were asleep telling and retelling the stories they'd heard about the West, dreaming of the life out ahead of them. I wonder if our congregations feel a little too permanent, too comfortable. Maybe we should go on a congregational camping trip or live in booths for a few days like the Jews do each year.

"He Is Coming Soon"

Our blessed hope has two parts—Jesus' Second Coming and our eternal heavenly home. I grew up in an era of prophecy conferences so we heard a lot about the Second Coming, but mostly so we'd know where it supposedly fit in God's grand scheme for the end times. I don't know that those meetings stirred my love and longing for Christ as much as they did my curiosity.

In general, we don't spend enough time dreaming of Jesus' return. Mentions of it are salted all through the New Testament, as if to say again and again, "Don't forget. Lift up your heads. He is coming soon." Scripture tantalizes us many times. Jesus said of the Son of Man, "He will send his angels and gather his elect from the four winds, from the ends of the earth to the ends of the heavens" (Mark 13:27). At the ascension the angels said, "Men of Galilee, why do you stand here looking into the sky? This same Jesus, who has been taken from you into heaven, will come back in the same way you have seen him go into heaven" (Acts 1:11). Paul made it all so vivid in 1 Thessalonians 4, "For the Lord himself will come down from heaven, with a loud command, with the voice of the archangel and with the trumpet call of God, and the dead in Christ will rise first. After that, we who are still alive and are left will be caught up together with them in the clouds to meet the Lord in the air. And so we will be with the Lord forever."

At the signal of the Father, Jesus Christ will rise from His sapphire throne and pass through the arches of glory, past the awesome living creatures who worship Him night and day, past the altar of sacrifice stained by His own blood and the altar of incense fragrant with the pleading prayers of His saints, and, summoning one great archangel to accompany Him, He will cross once again the great gulf fixed between heaven and earth, and step through the curtain of the sky. No need for a star to point Him out this time. No need for shepherds or wise men to spread the word. No disguises of baby flesh or swaddling clothes this time. As C. S. Lewis said, "When the author walks on to the stage, the play is over." This time there will be no mistaking His coming. "'Look, he is coming with the clouds' and 'every eye will see him.'"

Some joys are better cheered together than alone, and this is surely one of them. We need to give God's people occasions to dial up our anticipation, to all look in the same direction —up. In some quarters of evangelicalism, eschatological excesses of the past have caused this generation of pastors to keep future things at homiletical arms' length. We've become skittish about preaching on the end times. Sadly, our people are shortchanged from hearing vivid and compelling sermons or songs about Jesus' return. Even if we are confounded by some apocalyptic mysteries, we must be certain that we stir in our people a longing for Jesus to come back, anchored by Scripture.

I love the story Joe Stowell told in a sermon about the problem they have at the Shepherd's Home in Union Grove, Wisconsin. It's a Christian home for the mentally handicapped. These kids are taught about Jesus, and they're taught that He can come back at any time. The problem is that each day the children run to the window to see if this is the day Jesus will return. They just can't keep their windows clean!

We can imagine, perhaps, at least a shadow of what a reunion with our loved ones will be like, but we are stretched beyond our limits to grasp what it will be like to meet the Lord in the air. He to whom we've prayed and sung, the beloved Lord who has always been near but never seen. Our image of Him has always been earthbound—the Son of Man, sandals and robe, cross-fixed, or standing beside the rolled-away stone. But in that reunion moment, we shall see Him in His glory, and we shall contribute to that glory, more than all the angels of heaven, for we are those He has redeemed. The faith we have so carefully cultivated and guarded will no longer be necessary. Faith—being certain of things unseen—will be pointless, for we will see Him.

The faith we have so carefully cultivated and guarded will no longer be necessary. Faith—being certain of things unseen—will be pointless, for we will see Him.

We may not have considered how thrilled Jesus will be too. For He is also waiting now for that day. He yearns to be with us more eagerly than any bridegroom awaiting his bride. He will be more excited than anyone that His church is gathered to Him, that His wedding is at hand. At Lazarus's tomb, Jesus wept for the waiting, but He will wait no longer. I do not know if resurrection bodies have adrenaline, but this I know: no one in all that excited assembly of the saints and angels who meet the Lord in the air will be more thrilled than Jesus Himself.

So as Paul told the Thessalonians, "Encourage one another with these words" (1 Thess. 4:18).

The Place He Prepares for Us

But that's just the beginning of the end. Jesus told His devastated disciples the night before His death, "I am going there to prepare a place for you" (John 14:2). Jesus was the first human being to set foot in heaven, dressed in His glorified body. He is our pioneer in that land. In one sense, He returned to heaven as one returns home, but as a man He was the first human to set foot there. Had He not gone first, what would we do? Even if we were allowed into heaven, without Jesus being there to greet us, I don't think we'd ever be at home. Alexander Maclaren wrote over a hundred years ago, "Like some poor savages brought into a great city, or rustics into the presence of a king and his court, we should be ill at ease amidst the glories and solemnities of that future life unless we saw standing there our Kinsman, to whom we can turn, and who makes it possible for us to feel that it is home. Christ's presence makes heaven the home of our hearts."

Before we settle in, we have our wedding banquet to attend. The Father doesn't delay Jesus' coming because the arrangements aren't complete. I don't suppose it takes much effort or time in heaven to spread a banquet table—to pluck fruit from the trees of life, to gather heaven's manna, or pour heaven's wine. But heaven grows more beautiful by the day, for each day heaven echoes with more praise for the saving works of God—more testimonies, more lost sheep found and prodigals come home. I wonder if our bridegroom Jesus looks about the splendors of heaven while He waits for our coming and whispers, "More songs! More joy! More crowns! More white linen! More places at My table! My bride is coming!"

Cultivating Sacred Restlessness

Imagine a family living far from a homeland they have never seen. They have old picture albums to pore over. They have letters. From generation to generation, their family has passed on the stories of their King and Brother. They gather sometimes to sing the songs of His kingdom. They have refused to seek citizenship in the land where they wait. The flag of their unseen homeland hangs on the wall. From time to time, one or another receives the summons to come and their departure leaves the others with a sense of longing and joy.

How does a church cultivate that kind of sacred restlessness? How do we instill holy homesickness in our people?

Preach

To begin with, we preach on it. For example, preach a Lenten sermon series on Christ's second coming, drawing each Sunday on a different text, concluding with Jesus' own understated pre-enactment on Palm Sunday. Expositors working through a section of Scripture often come on texts that are tethered to Christ's return or our hope of heaven. Stop at those places to survey the grandeur with your people.

Lesslie Newbigin wrote, "The task of the church, and the task of the leader in the church, is to make this other world credible; to make it possible for men to believe that this world as it is, is not the last word; to keep constantly alight in men's hearts the flame of hope and faith in the possibility of a different kind of world."

Once, I took a preaching series idea from the chapters in a little book by Robert E. Coleman, *Songs of Heaven* (later reissued as *Singing with the Angels*). He simply focused only on the hymns in Revelation, making a more manageable series. The Colemans were part of our congregation so I asked his wife, Marietta, if these had come from sermons he had preached. "No," she said. "He wrote it during a very dark time in our lives. I think he wrote it," she continued, "so he wouldn't lose his mind."

Stories

Share stories from those whose hope of heaven carries them. If a story won't fit in with the focus of a Sunday morning, send it out to your church via email, newsletter, or a podcast. Call them "Dispatches from Home." Seek out stories not only from your own pastoral experience but from others'.

I've met with a small group of pastors for many years. One morning, two of my colleagues came dressed in suits because they each had a funeral that day, back to back, at the same funeral home. The first was for an elderly woman who had come to Christ as an adult and whose kids had known her both as a bad mom and good mom. But at this funeral, there would be gratitude for what Jesus had done in her life, and hope of a glad reunion.

The other funeral was for a godly woman in her thirties who died of cancer, leaving a husband and young children. When I asked him about the funeral later, Steve wrote:

> The sense of the funeral was one of real grief and yet genuine rejoicing over a life consumed with passion for the glory of God. So many of the people in her extended family are committed believers, the funeral was a true and real experience of worship. No one has any doubt but that one instant after Beth passed from this world last Sunday evening, she woke up in more glory and joy than any of us can possibly imagine right now.

Sing

Homesickness has long found expression and relief in songs about home. Slaves and soldiers, prisoners and pioneers, all have their homesick songs. Wars don't stir songs about battles, but rather songs about loved ones at home. Yet what was the last song you sang in your church about Jesus' return or heaven?

In an article for Desiring God Ministries, Matthew Westerholm wrote, "I recently compared two large selections of worship songs. The first was the most commonly sung congregational songs in the United States since the year 2000; the second was the most commonly published congregational songs from 1730–1850. Among many similarities, one difference was striking: *Our churches no longer sing about Christ's second coming as much as we used to.*"[2]

Whenever I preach on any text emphasizing our hope, we build our worship time around that theme. It can be a challenge to find songs, especially songs that our people know. We range all over, from hymns to gospel songs, spirituals to contemporary songs. Singing like that not only brings joy to that worship service but also equips our people for their future. In our darkest times, when we walk through the shadowy valley of death, we will search our memories for songs of hope to keep up our spirits, so we need to give people a repertoire now.

Quite often when I'm preaching on these themes, I put the sermon early in the service and leave plenty of time after to celebrate, shaped by the morning's text. We might space out the songs with quotes about heaven or a readers' theater piece drawn from one of Revelation's hymns. We've quoted excerpts from *The Pilgrim's Progress* and from C. S. Lewis. I recently heard a line we must use soon. Dr. Robert Smith Jr. spoke of the day "when we step on the other shore and wring the dark waters of our tribulations from our garments."

In Russell Banks's novel *Cloudsplitter*, written in the voice of one of the abolitionist John Brown's sons, he describes coming home after a long time away, only to find the old house empty. But then, he hears his family approaching. As I read this, I wondered if Banks was really describing a reunion in heaven.

> Suddenly, the empty vessel has been filled, and out of invisibility and silence, I have been made visible to myself, and audible! I call out to them, joyous and grateful for the simple fact of their existence elsewhere than in my mind and memory, and rush pell-mell from the house to the yard and greet them there. These beautiful, utterly familiar faces and bodies are real, are tangible!

And here, at last, clasped to the bosom of family and friends, I am one with others again! As when I was a child and my mother had not died yet. As when Father had not begun to block out the sun and replace it with his own cold disk, as when he had not cast me in his permanent shadow. They all touch me, and they even embrace me, and they say how glad they are to have me with them again. *Though nothing is forgotten, all is forgiven!*[3]

And If We Don't?

There is the sadly mistaken idea that thoughts of heaven are for the aged. There's no doubt that older Christians find great comfort in these things, but it is a terrible mistake to think that "our blessed hope" is only for those nearing death's border. None of the Bible's texts on these subjects appear in such a context. These passages are always given to encourage world-weary believers, to fortify those of whom the world is not worthy, to bring joy to the sad, and to loosen the vise grip some believers have on this world.

When Jesus' second coming and heaven are neglected, we lose the sense of being pilgrims and start to get too comfortable here. We become worldly and earthbound. Our theology wobbles, off-balance. To think little of Jesus' return is to think poorly of Jesus. And if we do not think on these things, we will not know how to encourage one another nor to die well.

To think little of Jesus' return is to think poorly of Jesus.

Several years ago I went to visit Belle in the care center. She was ninety-five, so we talked of heaven and I sang a heaven song for her.[4] On my way out I noticed another elderly lady I'd met on a previous visit. She was in her wheelchair in the common area. She smiled the most beautiful smile! The first time I saw her smiling I just *knew* she loved Jesus so I went over to meet her. Her name was Jesse Campbell, and she was ninety-three. Her husband of seventy-five years had died the year before. When I greeted her this time, she told me she was so excited because she would get to go home the next day.

"I bet you have a good church," I said, and she beamed.

"Trinity A.M.E. Church in Waukegan," she said proudly.

"What's your favorite hymn?" I asked. Without a moment's hesitation, she said, "Jesus Is All the World to Me." I got down on one knee and took her hand. "Let's sing it together," I said. "We'll see if we can remember the words." So there in that common room, with people coming and going around us, Jesse and I sang,

> *Jesus is all the world to me,*
> *My life, my joy, my all;*
> *He is my strength from day to day,*
> *Without him I would fall . . .*

After we finished the last words, "He's my friend," I stood to go. "If you're going home tomorrow," I said, "I might never see you again until we meet in heaven."

She nodded. "I'll see you there!" she said.

And so, somewhere in that white-robed multitude, freed forever from this world's withering heat and heartbroken tears, Belle and Jesse and I will meet again and sing of Jesus, just like we learned to do with our family back here.

To consider:

How would you describe your own thoughts about Christ's return and for our heavenly home?

How would you like to help your church long more earnestly for these things?

Afterword

Countless Christ-loving congregations feel like home. It really isn't so unusual but, make no mistake, each one is a gospel miracle. "Once you were not a people, but now you are the people of God" (1 Peter 2:10). Believers "are no longer foreigners and strangers, but fellow citizens with God's people and also members of his household, built on the foundation of the apostles and prophets, with Christ Jesus himself as the chief cornerstone" (Eph. 2:19–20).

Like earthbound families, we have our troubles from time to time. Some church families are graceless. Some are a disgrace. A friend told me once, "Religious mean is the meanest mean there is." Sadly, he had learned that from experience. Since churches are supposed to be families, they can break your heart. Ask any pastor. Ask those whose trust was betrayed. Ask those who weren't welcome or were mugged in a church fight.

But so many congregations are sweet and nourishing. They are safe and familiar. They are *home.* We learn to treasure them, not so much for our big events but for the everyday blessings of our lives together in Jesus. The songs we sing together, choir-like. The tentative beginnings of what become our most beloved friendships. The times we've prayed for one another, for work or kids or health. The prodigals we've ached to see again. The labors we've shared, the children who become all our children, the missionaries and outreaches we have taken on, our meals together. The pastors we've loved, the Sunday school teachers and youth leaders. The time elders gathered around one who was suffering, oil on a fingertip and faith in their hands. The old men and women, who were fathers and mothers to us, and who showed us aged grace. Babies dedicated or baptized. The heartbroken partings, buoyed by hope. Those precious times when Jesus drew so close to us we did not want to leave. As the nineteenth-century poet Eliza Cook wrote, "Sweet is the hour that brings us home."

Being a part of the family is in every Christian's spiritual DNA. There is no Christian anywhere who is not a brother or sister.

Those who lead a church family must shift from thinking of the church primarily as an organization to one that is God's family. For many of us, our values must change.

- Learn names and listen to stories

- Give serious attention to the spiritual, emotional, and physical care of God's people. In other words, "Be shepherds of God's flock that is under your care" (1 Peter 5:2).

- Lay off the relentless drive to grow bigger. "The Lord gives the increase." No family's worth is found in their size.

- Honor the aged as well as the young. God's people "will still bear fruit in old age, they will stay fresh and green," and young believers need to anticipate God's faithfulness through the years and the precious hope of heaven (Ps. 92:14).

- Eat together more often.

- Celebrate more frequently what God does among us.

- Pray together. People will much sooner eat together than pray together, so put it in a prime time. Be dogged in inviting them, one at a time, if need be. Don't give up. No church rises any higher than their praying.

- Call on the soul-sick and pursue the wayward, even before you pursue last week's visitors.

- Make disciples the slow way—in the church's family life. No disciple will be worth his or her salt who doesn't love their church family.

- Don't worry so much about being professional.

- Preach very well. It is how our Father speaks to His household.

- Remember your extended family—the big and small churches around you, the believers in faraway places, and especially those who are persecuted for their faith in Jesus Christ.

- Pray and lead as though *nothing* matters so much to Christ as this: "Love one another."

Through such things a church finds their identity as God's household. Those who come in will say, "God is really among you!" and when they see that these people really love one another, and they too feel loved, they may well feel homesick. And we'll be ready to welcome them.

Each year at Christmas we hear Mary, Joseph, and the babe referred to as "the holy family." But *we* are the holy family. We are the Father's children. We are Christ's bride. We are Jesus' brothers and sisters. We come to His table now as we will in heaven. We are *not* His organization. We are His family. He is at home among us as He was in the home of Mary, Martha, and Lazarus, for wherever two or three are gathered in His name, He is there in our midst. And when Jesus is in the midst of our church family, it feels like home.

Acknowledgments

A strong and positive sense of home is a grand gift. I'm thankful to my parents, Lyle and Grace, and my siblings, Linda and Larry, and also to my church families in South Dakota, Pennsylvania, and Illinois. So many good and gracious brothers and sisters. This way of thinking about church as home—this philosophy of ministry—has come from Scripture, to be sure, but also from serving Jesus and those congregations.

I live among scholars, being near Trinity Evangelical Divinity School, and I appreciate the quiet, painstaking work required of them in the service of us all. Three scholars in particular have helped my thinking in this book. Dr. Joseph Hellerman first opened my eyes to the significance of the New Testament's use of the language of brothers and sisters. Dr. Stephen Woodworth's work on Paul's view of pastoral leadership as parenting gave muscle to my own convictions. Dr. Lawson Younger, who is my friend and part of our church, opened my eyes to see the book of Ruth in a new way. His *NIV Application Commentary* on Judges and Ruth was my teacher.

I'm especially grateful to my sister, Anne Tohme, who co-wrote chapter 9, "What Care Looks Like." Also, for my fellow elders at Village Church of Lincolnshire who not only read parts of this book, but are helping me figure out how it all works. Ronnie and Corinna Waud let me use their wonderful pool house facing out to the sea for several very productive days of writing.

Then there are my editors. First, my wife, Susan, perceptive and patient with me, stuck with trying to figure out when I want constructive feedback and when I want straight up, unabridged affirmation. Acquisitions Editor Drew Dyck listened to this idea, launched me on my way, and kept me on track. Elizabeth Newenhuyse's extraordinary editorial skill made everything better. It's amazing to have someone give so much attention to my words.

And best of all, I acknowledge my Lord Jesus Christ, who is my Elder Brother and our heroic and loving Bridegroom. I am so grateful to be adopted into His family and I am eager for our endless ages together.

Notes

Introduction

1. Addie Zierman, "When Is It Time to Leave a Church?," *Faith Reimagined* (blog), March 30, 2016, https://addiezierman.com/2016/03/30/.

Part One—Our Family Album

1. Mary Schmich, "Passover Pang Brings a Taste of How Exclusion Feels," *Chicago Tribune*, April 21, 2000, https://www.chicagotribune.com/news/ct-xpm-2000-04-21-0004210294-story.html.

Chapter 1—You Can't Feel at Home in an Organization

1. Robert Banks, *Paul's Idea of Community: The Early House Churches in Their Historical Setting* (Grand Rapids: Baker, 1994), 50, 49.

2. Mark Buchanan (author, pastor, and professor), email message to the author, October 2018.

3. Marshall Shelley, "Vision and Values," CT Pastors Newsletter, October 20, 2017.

4. Victoria Taylor, "West Virginia Mom with 34 Children Explains Why She Isn't Done Adopting," *Daily News*, November 19, 2014, https://www.nydailynews.com/life-style/west-virginia-mom-shares-life-34-children-article-1.2016855.

5. J. D. Vance, *Hillbilly Elegy* (New York: HarperCollins Publishers, 2016), 150–51.

Chapter 2—Ruth: The Love That Will Not Let Us Go

1. K. Lawson Younger, *The NIV Application Commentary: Judges and Ruth* (Grand Rapids: Zondervan, 2002), 417.

2. Ibid., 393.

3. Ibid., 481.

Chapter 3—Brothers and Sisters

1. Nick Green, "Family Lost, Family Found: How Long-Lost Brothers, Sisters Were Discovered by South Bay Man," *Daily Breeze*, January 13, 2018, https://www.dailybreeze.com/2018/01/13/family-lost-family-found-a-south-bay-family-discovers-long-lost-brothers-sisters/.

2. Joseph H. Hellerman, *When the Church Was a Family: Recapturing Jesus' Vision for Authentic Christian Community* (Nashville: B&H Publishing, 2009), 50.

3. Dick Lukas & Christopher Green, *The Message of 2nd Peter & Jude (Bible Speaks Today)* (Downers Grove, IL: InterVarsity Press, 1995), 60.

4. "The Priorities, Challenges, and Trends in Youth Ministry," Barna, April 6, 2016, https://www.barna.com/research/the-priorities-challenges-and-trends-in-youth-ministry.

5. "5 Reasons Millenials Stay Connected to Church," Barna, September 17, 2013, www.barna.com/research/5-reasons-millennials-stay-connected-to-church.

6. Dave Ferguson and Matthew Soerens, "'Family Win' and How Our Church Care for Each Other and the World," *Christianity Today*, January 29, 2018, https://www.christianitytoday.com/edstetzer/2018/january/family-win-and-how-our-churches-care-for-each-other-and-wor.html.

Chapter 4—Love's Coat of Many Colors

1. St. Jerome, *Commentary on Galatians*, trans. Andrew Cain, Fathers of the Church Series (Washington, DC: The Catholic University of America Press, 2010), 260.

2. Lee Eclov, *Pastoral Graces: Reflections on the Care of Souls* (Chicago: Moody Publishers, 2012), 91–95.

3. Michael O. Emerson, "They're Playing Our Song: The Secret Multiracial Churches Know about Music," *Christianity Today*, June 22, 2012, https://www.christianitytoday.com/ct/2012/juneweb-only/multiracial-church-music.html. Review of Gerardo Marti, *Worship Across the Racial Divide: Religious Music and the Multiracial Congregation* (New York: Oxford University Press, 2012).

4. Terri Pous, "Ann Landers and Dear Abby," *Time*, January 3, 2013, http://newsfeed.time.com/2013/01/04/double-vision-top-10-famous-twins/slide/ann-landers-and-dear-abby/.

Chapter 5—Philemon: Fresh Starts Refresh Hearts

1. Quoted in Philip Yancey, *What's So Amazing about Grace?* (Grand Rapids: Zondervan, 1997), 15.

2. Joseph Hellerman, *When the Church Was a Family* (Nashville: B&H Publishing, 2009), 1–2.

3. Saint Ignatius, *The Epistles of St. Ignatius, Bishop of Antioch*, trans. J. H. Srawley (London: Macmillan Company, 1919), 39–40.

Part Two—Interior Design: The Spiritual Art of Decorating a Church Home

1. Netflix Original documentary series, *Abstract: The Art of Design,* "Ilse Crawford: Interior Design."

Chapter 6—God's Family at Rest

1. Paul Tournier, *A Place for You* (New York: HarperCollins, 1968), 9.

2. See Hosea 6:6; Matthew 9:13; 12:7.

3. Peter Walsh, *Lighten Up: Love What You Have, Have What You Need, Be Happier with Less* (New York: Free Press, 2011), 203.

4. Ed Stetzer, "One-on-One with Keith Getty on Congregational Singing in the Global Church," *The Exchange* (blog), July 7, 2018, https://www.christianity today.com/edstetzer/2018/july/one-on-one-with-keith-getty-on-congrega tional-singing-in-gl.html.

Chapter 7—Company's Coming

1. Fred Craddock, "When the Roll Is Called Down Here" (sermon), Preaching Today, https://www.preachingtoday.com/sermons/sermons/2010/july/ whentherolliscalleddownhere.html.

Chapter 8—Personal Attention

1. Eugene Peterson, *Five Smooth Stones for Pastoral Work* (Grand Rapids: Wm. B. Eerdmans Publishing Co, 1980), 5.

2. Excerpts from Lee Eclov, "Your Most Undervalued Role," *Leadership Journal,* April 2016.

3. North Point Community Church, http://northpoint.org/about.

4. Will Mancini, "North Point Community Church Strategy Imagery," https:// www.willmancini.com/north-point-community-church-strategy-imagery.

Chapter 9—What Care Looks Like

1. Eusebius, *Historia ecclesiastica* book 7, chapter 22; quoted in Joseph Heller-man, *When the Church Was a Family: Recapturing Jesus' Vision for Authentic Christian Community* (Nashville: B&H Publishing, 2009), 118.

Chapter 10—The Whole Church Preaches

1. Susan Walker, "Stories That Heal," a review of *Medicine Walk* by Richard Wagamese, published in the *Literary Review of Canada* (July–August 2014), https://reviewcanada.ca/magazine/2014/07/stories-that-heal/.

2. Richard Wagamese, *One Native Life* (Vancouver: Douglas & McIntyre, Ltd, 2008), 50–52.

3. Joseph Hellerman, *When the Church Was a Family: Recapturing Jesus' Vision for Authentic Christian Community* (Nashville: B&H Publishing, 2009), 105.

4. Mark Sayers, *Strange Days: Life in the Spirit in a Time of Upheaval* (Chicago: Moody Publishers, 2017), 141. Quoting Lesslie Newbigin, *A Word in Season: Perspectives on Christian World Missions* (Grand Rapids: Eerdmans, 1994), 153.

5. Ibid.,143.

6. Barbara Brotman, "Front Patio Makes a Great Hook if Fishing for People," August 3, 2009, https://www.chicagotribune.com/news/ct-xpm-2009-08-03-0908020296-story.html.

7. Barbra Brotman, "Sit-down Has People Talking in East Chicago" August 8, 2010, https://www.chicagotribune.com/living/ct-xpm-2010-08-09-ct-talk-brotman-benches-20100809-story.html.

8. Randy Frazee, *The Connecting Church: Beyond Small Groups to Authentic Community* (Grand Rapids: Zondervan, 2001), 163.

Chapter 11—Parenting the Church Family

1. Kevin A. Miller, "From Relevant Dude to Spiritual Father," *CT Pastors*, September 5, 2011, https://www.christianitytoday.com/pastors/2011/summer/spiritualfather.html.

2. Steve L. Woodworth, "How Pastors Can Reclaim the Role of Spiritual Parent," *CT Pastors*, June 2018, https://www.christianitytoday.com/pastors/2018/june-web-exclusives/in-dad-deprived-society-pastors-can-fill-that-role.html.

3. Tullian Tchividjian, *One Way Love: Inexhaustible Grace for an Exhausted World* (Colorado Springs: David C. Cook, 2013), 57.

4. *Preaching Today* illustration; from Larry Crabb, *Encouragement: The Key to Caring* (Grand Rapids: Zondervan, 1984), submitted by Alan Wilson, Nyon, Switzerland.

Chapter 12—Close to Home

1. Susan J. Matt, *Homesickness: An American History* (New York: Oxford University Press, 2011), 26–27.

2. Matthew Westerholm, "Come, Lord Jesus: The Simple Prayer Our Songs Forgot," Desiring God, April 17, 2016, https://www.desiringgod.org/articles/come-lord-jesus.

3. Russell Banks, *Cloudsplitter: A Novel* (New York: HarperCollins, 1998), 692.

4. For the story of my visit to Belle, see Lee Eclov, *Pastoral Graces: Reflections on the Care of Souls* (Chicago: Moody Publishers, 2012), 155.

About the Author

L ee Eclov has been a pastor in the Evangelical Free Church of America for forty years, serving five years as an Assistant Pastor in Deerfield, Illinois, fourteen years as Senior Pastor in Beaver Falls, Pennsylvania, and twenty-one years in Lincolnshire, Illinois. He is a native of South Dakota and the son of a rural church. He graduated from Trinity College and Trinity Evangelical Divinity School. Lee has contributed many articles to PreachingToday.com, *Leadership Journal*, CTPastors.com, and *Mature Living* magazine. He compiled *The Pastor's Service Manual* (NextStep Resources, 2012), and *Pastoral Graces: Reflections on the Care of Souls* (Moody Publishers, 2012), which was *Leadership Journal's* Book of the Year in the category The Leader's Inner Life. Lee is an adjunct professor at Trinity Evangelical Divinity School, teaching pastoral counseling. He and his wife, Susan, have been married forty-six years and have one grown son, Anders. To read some of Pastor Lee's articles go to www.leeeclov.com.

REFLECTIONS ON THE CARE OF SOULS

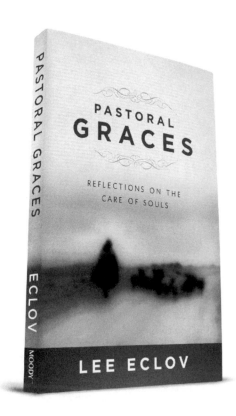

Resonating with every pastor, *Pastoral Graces* will reinvigorate grace in the churches they shepherd. Lee Eclov will equip the reader to understand their calling, their equipping, ministering in difficult circumstances and relationships, the mutual benefits for the congregation and the pastor, and how to finish well.

978-0-8024-0567-8 | also available as an eBook

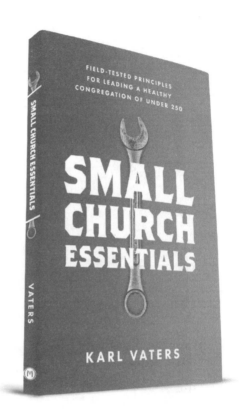

CATCH A. W. TOZER'S CONTAGIOUS PASSION FOR THE CHURCH OF CHRIST

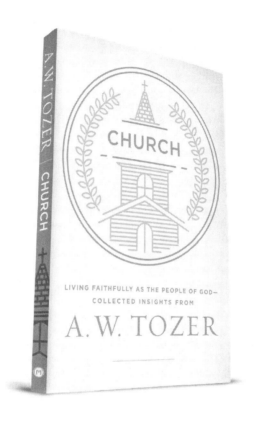

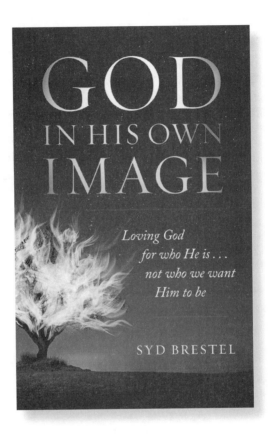